"Masterfully, Art McNeese use: of the beauty of God's grace on ᵥ theological issues to easy-to-understand concepts. He weaves a tapestry of helpful personal illustrations with each section ending in "Practical Secrets" to reinforce the chapter's lessons. The gospel of Jesus Christ is front and center in this biblically based message of salvation by grace alone. Laymen and Pastors will find *Making Space for Grace* instructive, enjoyable and helpful in applying God's *Amazing Grace*."

—Dr. Donald Brake, PhD, Dean Emeritus Multnomah Biblical Seminary. Author of *They Called Him Yeshua* and *Jesus, A Visual History*.

"Delightful! That's the word that comes to mind as I read Art McNeese's book on Grace. It's style is light and airy. We aren't talking about a cumbersome treatise on grace. This is a practical, inspiring attitude-changing book. It will lift your mind and soul. Art covers hard topics like salvation and overcoming shame, but never in a way that weighs on your soul. Quite the opposite, the grace that Art teaches liberates and elevates us out of our shame through the power of Jesus our Savior. The book is full of little boxes labeled "Practical Steps." These steps take the grace-laden transformation of our worldview and apply it to change both our emotions and our lifestyle. This grace that Art explains is the missing piece for our culture right now. We are turning against one another because our society knows nothing of grace."

—Greg Pruett, President of Pioneer Bible Translators and author of *Extreme Prayer*

"I've had the privilege of watching Art McNeese minister in his church, and I was struck at the time by two things: his sincere love for the people in his congregation, and the gentle grace he shows in the way he interacts with them. I am pleased to say that in "Making Space for Grace" those two qualities are on display and available for all his readers. Art gently teaches us how grace can transform us and draw us into deeper, more fulfilling relationships. You should make some space in your life for reading this book!"

—Matt Mikalatos, author of *Good News for a Change* and *Sky Lantern*

"Art McNeese skillfully uses Scripture and everyday situations to give a better picture of God's grace. He also provides practical tips for further study or accountability. This book is an excellent read from a man who exhibits a grace-filled life."

—Scotty Sanders, Author & Executive Director of Church Catalyst

"In *Making Space for Grace*, Art McNeese will saturate you with go-to biblical advice and decades of wisdom. As you turn each page you will benefit from his lifetime of pastoring, and be filled with inspiration, enlightenment, biblical teaching, and an understanding of the Father's love for you. When you are done, you will be, as Pastor Art puts it, "dancing in His freedom." If you want to deepen your relationship with Jesus Christ, and expand your understanding of grace, you'll love this book."

—Lucille Williams, author of *From Me to We*, and *The Intimacy You Crave*

"With fresh insight, Art McNeese explores the unique facets of grace and guides readers through life-changing applications of grace to Christian life. *Making Space for Grace* is a valuable resource for churches, Bible studies, small groups, and individuals desiring to grow in their faith."

—Shelly Beach
Christy, Selah, Reader's Favorite, and Golden Scroll Award Winner
Ambushed by Grace and other titles

"It is clear that Art has received grace from God and from others, because he has shown a tremendous amount of grace in his life and ministry. In *Making Space for Grace*, Art has captured the essence of what it means to live a life that is shaped by God's unmerited favor and love."

—Kyle Cunningham, Lead Minister, BridgeWay Church

MAKING
S P A C E
for
GRACE

A Believer's Guide to Living Out Grace

Art McNeese

WESTBOW
P R E S S®
A DIVISION OF THOMAS NELSON
& ZONDERVAN

WestBow Press books may be ordered through booksellers or by contacting:

WestBow Press
A Division of Thomas Nelson & Zondervan
1663 Liberty Drive
Bloomington, IN 47403
www.westbowpress.com
1 (866) 928-1240

ISBN: 978-1-9736-8921-8 (sc)
ISBN: 978-1-9736-8923-2 (hc)
ISBN: 978-1-9736-8922-5 (e)

Library of Congress Control Number: 2020905790

Print information available on the last page.

WestBow Press rev. date: 4/17/2020

This book is dedicated to my wife Holly, whose grace has blessed me immeasurably and whose love has consistently demonstrated the heart of Christ.

CONTENTS

FOREWORD

A story is told that the great Oxford don C.S. Lewis once walked in on a group of his colleagues as they were discussing major world religions.

"Dr. Lewis," they said, "What makes Christianity distinct from other world systems of faith?"

"That's easy," he responded. "It's grace."

It's often said that all the religions of the world are pretty much alike, but nothing could be further from the truth. All faiths except Christianity teach that people must work to achieve a relationship with God. Without exception, non-Christian religions teach that to reach a form of eternal life or transcendent experience with God, individuals must climb a ladder of performance to qualify.

Sixty-eight percent of born-again Christians in America believe that the saying "God helps those who help themselves" is a verse that comes from the Bible. But not only is this phrase not found in the Bible, it contradicts what the Bible teaches about grace. Grace says that God helps those who realize they can't save themselves.

Sadly, Christianity is often represented as another form of do-it-yourself salvation. This erroneous concept suggests to Christians that our position with God is predicated on our success in always "getting it right." And what is "it"?

Obeying all the rules.

Qualifying by way of our spiritual competence or excellence.

Continually pursuing a goal that our self-centered propensities are incapable of achieving.

The result of such teaching is devastating. Believers are led to believe that their standing before God is the product of their own moral goodness or their correctness in every detail of theology. No wonder so many believers end up giving up on faith, because they realize that they can never measure up.

A Christianity that fails to make space for grace deters non-Christians from committing their lives to Christ. Some people refuse to believe because they consider themselves "good enough" to be saved. These individuals operate on the premise that achieving a relationship with God is based on a performance "scale." They assume that their good works are more impressive than other people's. Why would they need Christ? For other non-believers, the barrier is just the opposite—they reason that they could never be "good enough," so they reject Christianity outright. After all, they can never chin the bar, so what's the use in trying?

This is why, when I share my faith with other believers, I always begin with grace. Christians often need to be disabused of the notion that their relationship with God depends on their performance. Otherwise, they believe their walk with Christ is fragile and tenuous, and they can never truly be certain of their salvation. (Of course, other people need to be reminded of the demands of grace so they don't presume on grace).

When I share my faith with non-believers, I also begin with grace. I've discovered that this concept disarms many would-be Christians. When it dawns on them that following Christ is not a matter of qualifying, but being qualified because of faith in Christ, a light comes on and they become more ready to become a disciple. In my experience, the single most common hurdle for non-Christians to overcome is their mistaken belief that to become a Christian, they have to "dot every i and cross every t" and live a perfect life. How sad that many who might otherwise choose to follow Jesus refuse to do so because they've believed a distorted concept of Christianity!

I wrote this book because I want believers to embrace the grace of God and to be changed by it. I want non-believers to get past the myth that to be eligible for salvation, they must prove themselves "good enough."

May God give us all the grace to accept and understand His free gift of grace!

INTRODUCTION

I grew up doing all the things Christians do. I went to church every Sunday. Check. I memorized the books of the Bible. Check. I went to summer Bible camp and sang all the songs about Jesus. Check. I committed my life to Christ at a young age and was baptized. Check. Through my middle school and high school years, I kept my spiritual nose clean (for the most part). Check. But I still felt an empty, hollow feeling deep inside that signaled that something was missing.

I attended a Christian university and received a theology degree. I could quote verses and speak on subjects like faith and salvation and what it meant to have a relationship with Christ. I had been introduced to the all-important subject of grace. But the reality of grace was still not part of my daily life. I possessed "head knowledge" about grace, but grace had not moved from my head to my heart. I was like a doctor who could prescribe the right medication but who had never taken medicine himself. I understood grace as a concept, but not a reality.

How does a Christian move from a theory of grace to living a life of grace? I've known thousands of people who could say the right things but who seemed to lack an internalized reality of grace.

For instance, consider a man who still doubts his salvation, in spite of his commitment to Christ and his remarkable generosity. He's made millions in his lifetime and given most of it away to the church and Christian causes. When I look at his life, I see one of God's great servants. But when I talk with him, he expresses honest doubts about his salvation. He's skeptical about his place in heaven and questions whether he's truly saved.

There's the woman who went through two failed marriages followed by numerous relationships with other men. She's since turned from her wrong choices and given her heart and life to Christ, but she still harbors concerns about her relationship with Christ. She acknowledges that God is a God of grace, but she believes that His grace applies to everyone but her.

Or how about the young man who is learning about Christ for the first time? I've presented the doctrine of grace to him again and again in our conversations. I've tried to help him see that following Christ isn't about achieving, but receiving. Still, he won't take the step to commit to Christ because he harbors the misconception that before he can become a Christian, he must get everything in his life "just right."

How do you learn to experience grace in the deepest part of your soul? How do you move grace from your head to your heart? If you believe in Christ but still have doubts about your salvation, this book is for you. This book is also for people who struggle to believe in Christ because they're convinced that a relationship with Him depends on their ability to achieve and perform.

Although you may give mental assent to the reality of God's grace, do you live in the shackles of what I call "un-grace"? Do you concede that there's nothing you can do to earn your salvation, but find yourself on a treadmill, constantly trying to prove yourself to God?

Do you enthusiastically sing "Amazing Grace" ("I once was lost, but now I'm found..."), but you still feel lost and alone?

Do you agree that you're saved by grace but find it impossible to live with grace in your marriage? Are you and your spouse in a downward spiral of gracelessness toward each other?

Do you recognize that you're saved by grace, but there's no way in the world you're willing to extend grace to the people who have wounded you? Have you been rescued by God's grace? Maybe. Are you willing to grant grace to your adversary? Forget it.

Do you celebrate that you are saved by grace, but your celebration never culminates in service to Christ and others? Do you appreciate being a recipient of grace, but that grace never overflows in giving to those in need?

Do you say grace at the dinner table, but your prayers seem hollow and sterile? Do you long for your conversations with God to be oiled with grace, but you frankly have no desire to spend time with Him?

Have you heard sermons on grace but have no interest in becoming a Christian? Does following Christ seems like an exercise for people who have it "all together" and you feel light years away from that goal?

Grace seems like an attractive theological concept, but you don't feel the flow of God's grace in your heart. You robotically serve Christ, but your walk with God is devoid of joy. You can paint by numbers, but you're deathly afraid of coloring outside the lines. You've learned salvation's dance steps, but there's no freedom or rhythm in your movement with God.

I have good news! You can move from mechanical assent to genuine delight in your grace experience. In the pages ahead, I will share the secrets of making space for grace. I'll guide you through what the Bible reveals about grace, and I'll give you practical suggestions about how to internalize grace and find yourself dancing in His freedom.

Part One

GRACE: MOVING FROM THEOLOGY TO REALITY

CHAPTER ONE

"Your worst days are never so bad
that you are beyond the reach of God's grace.
And your best days are never so good
that you are beyond the need of God's grace."
—Jerry Bridges

BELLY FLOPS

Have you ever thought of yourself as a mutant—someone who doesn't belong? Someone who doesn't fit in, isn't good enough, and is unlike everyone else?

Kind of like a mutant.

Let me explain with a story. A few years ago, my wife Holly and I visited the Jelly Belly® factory in California. This factory makes the Cadillac version of jellybeans—only the finest. Jellybean murals of Ronald Reagan decorate the walls, commemorating the President who kept a jar of jelly beans on his desk in the Oval Office. Another mural features a jellybean tribute to Elvis.

But to understand this story, you need to know something about Holly. She loves candy of all varieties, but she has a special fascination with "mutants," such as misshapen Mike and Ikes and deformed Hot Tamales. Holly is drawn to any piece of candy that bears a defect. (Don't ask me why. I still don't understand.)

We toured the factory, then reached the final attraction—the store where the public could buy Jelly Bellies. We were surprised to discover ten-pound bags of beans labeled "Belly Flops." Sadly, these beans hadn't made the final cut by Jelly Belly inspectors. Some were discolored. Some were oddly shaped. Others lacked the sheen you normally find on Jelly Bellies.

Holly was delighted by this discovery! She could not only purchase Jelly Bellies at a discount price, but also buy bags filled with the rejects, the abnormal, and the slightly weird. These candies weren't good enough to meet Jelly Belly standards. Belly Flops were designated as failures. They were tossed aside. Flops. An embarrassment to all authentic Jelly Bellies.

Isn't that often how we feel about ourselves? Flops. Rejects. Defective. Because we live in a shame-based culture, we feel like flops. Shame and rejection seep into our hearts. We're hungry for grace, but we struggle to find it in our world.

Lewis Smedes identifies three sources of crippling shame that make us feel like flops:[1]

> Secular culture
> Graceless religion
> Unaccepting parents

Secular culture can make us feel like flops. From nursery school on, we're taught that we are what we achieve. Schools rank students according to their test scores and GPAs. Shame-based parenting, trauma, and abuse can often produce negative coping behaviors like anorexia, substance abuse, and self-harm. These reactions also result from a culture that screams that teenage girls and women must look like beautiful, emaciated models. Our culture makes it challenging for us to feel good about ourselves because no matter how much we achieve, someone will always be better than we are. Our culture is filled with voices shouting, "You aren't good enough! You're a flop!"

PRACTICAL SECRET: Drench yourself in Bible passages that affirm God's unconditional love for you. Remember: there are no strings attached to God's love for you. His love for you isn't contingent on you getting it all right. He just loves you, period. Plaster this text on your dashboard, your bathroom mirror, and your office computer screen: "But God showed His great love for us by sending Christ to die for us while were still sinners" Romans 5:8.

Toxic religion can also make us feel like flops. Some people won't go to church because religion sometimes points a bony finger of indictment in people's faces and says, "Let me tell you what a bad person you are!"

We don't simply feel bad about our behavior; we perceive ourselves as defective and worthless human beings. If life is like the Jelly Belly assembly line, we see ourselves as rejects on God's conveyor belt.

"Why would God want to hear from someone like me?" we might think. "I don't come close to living up to His standards. He can't want me."

You've tried hard to be good—to do the right thing, only to fail for the ten-thousandth time. God forgave you 9,999 times, but for some reason you think this time tipped the scales, and you're a flop.

Parents sometimes make us feel like flops. Many people have loving and caring parents. But sometimes parents unintentionally or intentionally communicate a lack of acceptance and even outright rejection to their kids.

I spoke with a man who told me, "In all of my forty-something years, my parents have never told me, 'Good job, son.'" One woman said she'd been on a long guilt trip, with her mom as the travel agent. Philip Yancey tells of a little girl who wanted to play perfectly in her first piano recital, so she practiced until her fingers were sore. At the recital, she performed flawlessly. But when she came back to her seat, her mom leaned over and whispered, "Your slip was showing."[2] Of course, the child felt she'd flopped.

> PRACTICAL SECRET: Surround yourself with people who show you grace. This doesn't mean spiritual yes-men: people who flatter you and overlook your faults. You must have individuals who affirm you and demonstrate that they are for you, no matter what. Have people in your life who love you with no strings attached.

In my office, I often hear from people who've been labeled flops. For instance, a woman who's been through a divorce and figures she's forever "damaged goods." The teenager who had an abortion and bears the stigma and pain of her decision. A man who said to me, "I have too much baggage to ever be good enough to go to church." And the brokenhearted young man whose father marched onto the football field and berated him for not making the tackle.

SKEWED PERSPECTIVE OF GOD

A skewed perspective of God can also make it difficult to accept grace. We may see God as someone who dangles us over the fires of hell waiting for us to slip up. We may envision Him as a Gestapo who can't wait to zap us in the gas chamber. Some people picture God as a motorcycle cop hiding behind a billboard, waiting to nab us for the least offense. Mess up, and He'll get you. In fact, He scans the earth looking for flops.

This flawed perspective can result from faulty and toxic preaching and teaching; for instance, religious people sometimes characterize God as a menacing brute instead of a loving Father. Some people erroneously project human traits on God. For instance, we know that others would never forgive us if they knew our faults, so we often assume that God responds the same way. This line of thinking often stems from a culture that constantly screams, "You are what you accomplish!"

I have a friend whose twenty-one-year-old addicted daughter was living in San Antonio with a man who abused her. Desperate, she called her father and said, "Dad, I want to come home." Of course, my friend rented a truck and drove to the Alamo City, but when he got there, she changed her mind. He pleaded with her for three hours to come home, but she wouldn't do it. So he returned to Dallas.

Three days later, she called him. "Dad, you're right. I should have come home. Would you come get me?"

"I can't come right now, but I'll rent you a truck and you can pack up your things and come home."

She packed her things and began the drive home, but when she got to Austin, she backed out. She turned around and went back to San Antonio. Over and over, my friend's daughter has promised to leave drugs and alcohol. She's changed her mind and left her dad in tears again and again. But do you think he loves her any less?

Not at all. Nothing she does will ever keep him from loving her. If my friend can love *his* daughter that much, think how much more God loves *us*!

You may sometimes feel that God could never love you because you've messed up so often. Remember: you can't ever do anything to make God love you more or make Him love you less. He loves you. Unconditionally. Period.

People try all kinds of things to earn God's love. Some people try restitution. "If I try to undo the wrong I've done, maybe God will love me." Restitution is good, but it can't earn anyone God's love.

Some people try contrition. "If I feel sorry enough for what I've done, maybe then God will love me." Contrition is commendable, but it doesn't earn anyone God's love.

Some people envision a spiritual balance sheet. "If I do enough good things to make up for the bad things I've done, maybe then God will love me." Doing good things is noble, but good works can't earn anyone God's love. God doesn't say, "I love you because ..." He doesn't say, "I love you if ..." or "I love you provided that ...". He says, "I love you." No strings attached.

Larry Crabb tells about a man who told Crabb about his childhood. The man was raised in an angry family. Mealtimes were miserable. Every meal was either silent or sarcastically cutting. But down the street a happy family lived in an old-fashioned house with a big porch. When the man was ten years old, he'd excuse himself from the dinner table. Then he walked to the old-fashioned house down the street.

If he got there during dinnertime, he crawled under the porch and listened to the family's laughter. Crabb listened intently, then said, "Imagine what it would have been like if the father in the house knew you were huddled beneath the porch. Imagine that the father in the happy house had invited you in. Imagine what it would have been like if you had been invited to sit at the table. Think about what it would have been like if you had spilled your glass of water. And imagine what it would have been like to hear the father say, "Get him more water! And a dry shirt! I want him to enjoy the meal!"[3]

God is the Father who invites us to the table—messes and all.

When people have a wrong view of God, they have a hard time accepting grace. They see a mean, harsh, vindictive caricature of God when nothing could be further from the truth.

PRACTICAL STEP: If you're married, commit yourself to be a grace dispenser, no matter what. You may be in a relationship where you receive little or no grace. This is challenging; however with the Holy Spirit's help, you can practice a grace-filled life. As you dispense grace, you will discover an enriched understanding of God's grace!

FLOPS LOVED BY GOD

We're all flops! But no matter how messy your background or misshapen your life, God wants you to embrace His love. Are you struggling with addiction and trying to find your way back to God? He loves you. Are you in trouble with the law and don't know where to turn? God loves you. Do you have doubts about whether God exists? God loves you. Have you been stigmatized by others because of sin in your life? God loves you.

Acceptance isn't based on our track record. It's based on Jesus' track record. The family of God is a place of grace: it's where we accept each other, because nobody has an edge on anyone else.

Some people won't accept Christianity because they think they could never be good enough. But if we think Christianity is about proving how good we are, we've missed the point. Christianity is about admitting how weak we are and asking for God's grace.

Other people think, *I could never become a Christian because I can't stand people who think they're better than everyone else.* Yes, some people who call themselves Christians are arrogant, but most don't see themselves as better than anyone else.

I listened as a Christian man confessed his struggle with pornography. He was broken and ashamed. The Christian men around the table said, "We want you to know that there's not a man here who feels an ounce of condescension." They didn't gloat: they prayed for him and urged him to partner with the Holy Spirit to root out this sin from his life.

In one sense, all of us are flops. No one can stand up to a flawless standard. We all have imperfections. Flaws. We're all misshapen. Big flops may have marked your life. You will still make mistakes along the way: foolish decisions, bad choices. You'll flop because we *all* do.

But the good news is that God loves flops. He loves us even when we fail and when we fall on our faces.

PRACTICAL STEP: Buy a handful of Belly Flops (just go to jellybelly. com) and keep them in a plastic bag. Carry them with you at all times. Label the outside of the bag "God loves flops."

Romans 5:8 says, "While we were still sinners Christ died for us." (NIV) God's grace is designed for all the flops of the world ... you and me. So when you begin to doubt that God loves you, think of a Jelly Belly Flop. Their imperfections don't make them valueless. Remember, no matter your flaws, God still loves you and gives you His grace. Yes, *you*, with all your failures and sins. God doesn't look on you and see a mutant or a reject. He sees someone who is infinitely valuable in His sight!

CHAPTER TWO

"The bridge of grace will bear your weight, brother.
Thousands of big sinners have gone across that bridge, yea,
tens of thousands have gone over it.
Some have been the chief of sinners and some have come
at the very last of their days but the arch has never yielded
beneath their weight. I will go with them trusting to the same support.
It will bear me over as it has for them."
–Charles Spurgeon

TREADMILLS

When I decided to deliver my Sunday message standing on a treadmill, I had no idea it would create enormous stress. Not for me, but for one of my listeners. I chose to speak from a treadmill to illustrate the fact that people try to "sweat" their way into a relationship with God. For one man present that day, the illustration didn't prevent sweat—it created it!

Bill Rogers was an affable grey-haired guest at our church who had a great sense of humor. He watched and listened as I described my experience during a stress test in the doctor's office.

"You start with a leisurely stroll. But after a few minutes, the tech hits a dial, and suddenly you're not walking. You're running and sweating just to keep up with the nasty machine."

As I spoke, I turned up the speed on the treadmill, and soon I was jogging. Right about that time I noticed an older gentleman crumple to the floor. Church members hustled him to another room while a doctor in attendance called an ambulance, which quickly delivered Bill to the hospital.

The next morning when I went to visit him, he joked about the incident. "I think I had a case of 'sympathetic treadmill syndrome.' As you were working out, I was transported back to my doctor's office, where I've undergone several stress tests.

"I've had preachers put me out (to sleep), but never one who almost put me under."

Bill's experience drilled home my point. Many people suffer from spiritual treadmill syndrome, constantly working to get closer to God, but they're not going anywhere! No one can ever do enough or be good enough to earn their way to God. Just when they think they're managing the speed, somebody turns up the machine.

Do you ever feel like you're working hard for God's approval, but not getting anywhere? Maybe you've tried getting on the treadmill. You've worked hard for God, but it seemed pointless. Why keep running when you aren't making any progress? So you decided to trade your treadmill for a Lazy Boy. Someone said: "Two things are true of a person trying to work his way to heaven. First, he's very busy. Second, he's very frustrated."

If we have a treadmill approach to our faith, we'll end up discouraged and disillusioned. This is because a treadmill approach traps us in a performance mentality. And sooner or later, we figure out that we can't perform perfectly. We can't keep up on the treadmill.

David Seamands wrote a book about the treadmill trap. Observe some of the letters he received:

> "I have been a struggling Christian for the past thirteen years. My problem is that I am never at peace and am always trying to be good—that is, to be better. I am so afraid of making mistakes."

> "I am a college student and a believer in Christ. Your article really hit home to me. I am always feeling that kind of anxiety, guilt, and condemnation. These feelings invade my day-to-day thought processes. I cannot perform a task, read a book, or practice my music without feeling I am being judged ... I feel everything I do is not good enough for my Lord."

"I try hard to be loving, but I'm so critical and judgmental, so hard on my spouse and kids. The slightest failure on their part and I get angry and explode. Then I feel guilty and get depressed. My family is so loving and forgiving— but that only makes matters worse. It's almost like a pattern that keeps repeating itself."

"It seems the harder I try, the harder I fall. When I get exhausted and quit trying, I feel condemned."[4]

So how do we get off the treadmill? What do we need to have a healthy relationship with God? Healthy relationships with others? The only way to get off the treadmill of performance is to accept and apply God's grace. Learn to reject negative self-talk that ignites a "I-have-to-get-it-right" mentality in your heart. Rehearse the narrative of God's goodness and your security in Him. Embrace the reality of God's refusal to ever give up on you!

PRACTICAL SECRET: Find two or three people with whom you can be completely transparent–people who know your ugly sins and most catastrophic failures. They've never betrayed you. These are your "grace buddies." Spend time with them. Lots of time. Their love for you mirrors God's love for you.

BELIEVING AND RECEIVING, NOT ACHIEVING

The crucial foundation of grace is *believing and receiving, not achieving.* Here's how Paul puts it in Romans Chapter 4: "If you're a hard worker and do a good job, you deserve your pay; your wages are not a gift. But if you see that the job is too big for you, that it's something only *God* can do, and you trust him to do it—you could never do it for yourself no matter how hard and long you worked—well, that trusting-him-to-do-it is what gets you set right with God, by God. Sheer gift." (Romans 4:4-5, *The Message*)

Grace is not something we earn. It's something we receive. And when God gives us his grace, he gives us *all* of his grace. We don't receive grace from God and then have to work to receive more. Remember when Oprah Winfrey gave away cars on her show? She gave all 276 of her audience members brand new cars. But when people went to pick up their new vehicles, they found out they had to pay several thousand dollars in taxes. The "gifted" car was classified as income. So was the car free? Yes and no. It was given without cost, but the new owners still had to pay taxes on the gift.

God doesn't give us salvation and then say, "Oh, I forgot to tell you: my grace is free and comes at no cost to you, but you still owe." When God gives us salvation, he pays for *everything*! We don't have to do anything to earn his gift of grace. In fact, that's the definition of grace: the unmerited, unearned favor of God!

Most people understand this when they first become Christians. They think, "Wow, salvation is great. I give my sin to God, and he gives me forgiveness and healing. It's free. I don't earn my way into heaven or pay a price. It's a free gift." But as time passes, they start thinking, "*This is too good to be true. I need to do something to earn his goodness to me.*" Then they step back on the treadmill.

This is exactly what the Galatians did. Paul came to Galatia and preached salvation by grace through faith. He taught that we can never do anything to earn God's favor. All we can do is receive it. The Galatians said yes to that offer. They put their trust in Christ for salvation. But then, they started backpedaling. People came into the Galatian church teaching salvation by merit, salvation by works. Paul was stunned!

Look at what Paul wrote: "How did your new life begin? Was it by working your heads off to please God? Or was it by responding to God's Message to you? Are you going to continue this craziness? For only crazy people would think they could complete by their own efforts what was initiated by God. If you weren't smart enough or strong enough to begin it, how do you suppose you could perfect it? Did you go through this whole painful learning process for nothing? It is not yet a total loss, but it certainly will be if you keep this up!" (Galatians 3:3-4, *The Message*)

Paul reminds the Galatians, You started out so well! You realized you couldn't save yourselves. You knew achieving could never get you to heaven. You believed that what Jesus did on the cross was enough to save you! But now you've regressed. You've fallen back into that old way of thinking. You've let somebody persuade you that *maybe* you can achieve salvation. You've fallen back into the treadmill trap, into a performance mentality. But even if you prayed every moment of your life, gave every penny you ever earned, and gave yourself tirelessly to ministry, you could never do enough to merit salvation.

What is *your* plan for getting to heaven? By receiving and believing, or by achieving? If you think getting to heaven comes by achieving, you're on the treadmill. You're straining and sweating and striving to measure up. You're not getting anywhere, and sooner or later, you'll collapse in exhaustion.

Elyse Fitzpatrick writes about the history of the treadmill: "In Victorian England, treadmills weren't found in air-conditioned health clubs—they were found in prisons. Treadmills, or tread wheels, as they were called, were used in penal servitude as a form of punishment. Some tread wheels were productive, grinding wheat or transporting water, but others were purely punitive in nature. Prisoners were punished by walking up an inclined plane day after day, knowing that their hard labor was for nothing.

"The only hope the prisoner had was that, at some day in the future, he would have 'paid his debt' to society and would be set free. He couldn't even look on his labor at the end of the day and know that, if nothing else, he'd been productive."[5]

As you struggle with sin, remember that Christ has set you free indeed and that you're no longer chained to the treadmill of sin and failure. He paid the ransom demanded for your release from sin, and you now walk in the freedom of the glory of the sons and daughters of God.

God offers you an invitation: Get off the treadmill and find peace in Him.

CHAPTER THREE

"I once thought these things were valuable, but now I consider them worthless because of what Christ has done. Yes, everything else is worthless when compared with the infinite value of knowing Christ Jesus my Lord. For his sake I have discarded everything else, counting it all as garbage, so that I could gain Christ and become one with him."
–The Apostle Paul

EXCHANGES

EXCHANGING PERFECTIONISM FOR PEACE

When we accept and apply God's grace, several great exchanges take place. First, we exchange *perfectionism* for *peace*. Romans 5:1-2 says, "Therefore, since we have been justified through faith, we have peace with God through our Lord Jesus Christ, through whom we have gained access by faith into this grace in which we now stand." (NIV) What does Paul mean by peace? Two things.

First, he refers to objective peace. Before we knew Christ, we were God's enemies, but now we're his friends. Romans 5:10 states, "For since our friendship with God was restored by the death of his Son while we were still his enemies, we will certainly be saved through the life of his Son." (NLT) We were archenemies of God. Our sins violated His holiness and assaulted His goodness.

But God took the initiative and restored the friendship. He offered His Son as the payment for our wrongs so that we're no longer adversaries. We're friends! God restored objective peace between Himself and us.

He destroyed the barrier that stood between us. Colossians 1:19-20 states, "For God was pleased to have all his fullness dwell in him, and through him to reconcile to himself all things, whether things on earth or things in heaven, by making peace through his blood, shed on the cross." (NIV)

Second, Paul is referring to subjective peace. We can have the peace *of* God because we now have peace *with* God. As long as we are estranged from God, we can never experience inner peace. We are tormented because we realize that our sins stand between God and us. We can never be at ease about our relationship with Him because deep inside we know that our sin makes friendship impossible. But when Christ went to the cross, He not only created objective peace, He gave us subjective peace. We can have peace in our hearts because we know without a doubt that not a trace of animosity exists between us. We're transformed from enemies to friends!

Perhaps you believe your identity is determined by how well you perform. Urban Meyer coached the University of Florida to the national football title in 2007. He grew up in a home with a dad who was extremely demanding and whose love was conditional. In 2009, Urban Meyer's winning streak came to an end. He suffered severe chest pains. He was found on the floor of his house, unable to move or speak. Meyer later confessed that he was driven by perfectionism. In part, his identity was based on how his team was doing. We sometimes do the same.

We often think, *If I can do enough "right things," I'll establish my value. My identity consists of the sum of my achievements. If I do well, I prove that I am somebody.* And if we don't succeed, we see ourselves as failures and believe that people who know us do too.

How tragic that contemporary culture reinforces this thinking to the point that we worship achievement.

PRACTICAL STEP: Picture yourself standing before Jesus in heaven. Imagine Him speaking these sentences to you: "Well done, good and faithful servant." "You are my forever child." "Nothing can separate you from my love." "It was never about your merit—it was always about my mercy."

EXCHANGING RULE-KEEPING
FOR RELATIONSHIP

There's a second great exchange. When we accept and apply God's grace, we exchange *rule keeping* for *relationship*. Paul was the ultimate law-keeper. He had a spiritual resume that could overshadow anyone else's. Paul had mastered the treadmill; he was disciplined to the core. But striving left him empty and devastated. He finally gave up the grind of the treadmill and embraced grace. When he did, Paul realized that moral living and doing the right thing were worthy goals, but he recognized that his scrupulous rule keeping was futile for securing his salvation!

Paul finally realized that he couldn't base his salvation on performance and rule keeping! He testifies that he was the poster child for rule keeping. He was passionate about keeping the law. He stayed on the treadmill. But then he realized how worthless those things were compared to knowing Christ. He dumped his legalistic lists in the trash. He didn't want superficial righteousness based on keeping rules. He wanted a robust righteousness that comes from trusting Christ!

Grace is far more demanding than law could ever be. A massive difference exists between legalism and love. Love does things law could never do. When Holly and I got married, I liked a lot of things about my old bachelor pad. It sported a pool table with a neon light suspended from the ceiling that created the ambience of a bar. Smoked mirrors graced the walls. The floor was covered with shag carpet from the seventies. The apartment boasted an avocado green fridge with funky fungus inside. I was proud of my grungy game room and didn't want to change the decor for anything.

Except love.

When I fell in love, everything changed. The pool table went. The smoked mirrors came down. The shag carpet was quickly replaced. I even gave up my treasured avocado green fridge for a white one. I did it all for the love of my life.

If we could comprehend a scintilla of God's unfathomable love and grace for us, we'd willingly do anything for Him. Grace is not about rule keeping! It's about relationship!

Paul knew that God had given him mercy and grace. Mercy, because God no longer counted his sins against him. And grace, because God not only forgave his sins—He gave him gifts far beyond anything Paul could have imagined.

So why do so many people depend on rules to get them to heaven instead of grace? They simply cannot imagine a God of mercy and grace. They think God only loves people who keep the rules.

Over the decades, adult Christians have said to children: "God loves good little boys and girls." But the truth of Scripture is that God loves boys and girls (and everyone). We tend to think that God loves "good" people, and if we're not good, then God doesn't love us! When we finally realize God loves us no matter what, we trade rule keeping for relationship. This is exactly what Paul did. He dumped all of his endeavors to win God's love by his own effort.

When you grasp grace, there's nothing you won't do for God! But you won't live for Him out of a sense of obligation: you're compelled to live for Him because you delight in a loving relationship with Him!

PRACTICAL STEP: When you know you have sinned, run toward God and not away from Him. Picture Jesus waiting with open arms to receive you. Visualize God throwing you a party and welcoming you. Again and again and again.

EXCHANGING LEGALISM FOR LOVE

The third great exchange effected by grace is trading *legalism* for *love*. Now what do I mean by legalism? Legalism motivates us when we try to earn God's approval through rules. But here's the irony: Legalism lowers God's standards. Legalism is deviously deceptive. It appears to be motivated by dedication to the highest possible standards. But the opposite is actually true.

The effect of making lots of rules and measuring people by how well they keep those rules is counterproductive. This is why religious people can be some of the harshest people in the world. This is why Jesus' heart broke when he saw people who looked all right on the outside, when they were actually all wrong on the inside. Legalism results in cosmetic differences, but love changes our hearts.

Ray Ortlund put it this way: "We were married to Mr. Law. He was a good man, in his way, but he did not understand our weakness. He came home every evening and asked, 'So, how was your day? Did you do what I told you to? Did you make the kids behave? Did you waste any time? Did you complete everything I put on your To Do list?' So many demands and expectations. And hard as we tried, we couldn't be perfect. We could never satisfy him. We forgot things that were important to him ... We failed in other ways. It was a miserable marriage, because Mr. Law always pointed out our failings. And the worst of it was, he was always right! But his remedy was always the same: Do better tomorrow. We didn't, because we couldn't.

"Then Mr. Law died. And we remarried, this time to Mr. Grace. Our new husband, Jesus, comes home every evening and the house is a mess, dinner is burning on the stove ... Still, he sweeps us into His arms and says, 'I love you, I chose you, I died for you, I will never leave you nor forsake you.' And our hearts melt. We don't understand such love. We expect him to despise us and reject us and humiliate us, but he treats us so well. We are so glad to belong to him now and forever, and we long to be "fully pleasing to him!" (Col.1:10) Being married to Mr. Law never changed us. But being married to Mr. Grace is changing us deep within, and it shows."[6]

This is the difference between legalism and love. Love does things for their beloved that law could never do! If we could grasp how much God loves us and how massive His grace is for us, we'd willingly do anything for Him. God is the great lover of His children, always pursuing us, always romancing us! The biblical narrative from beginning to end reveals that God loves us, and He wants us to love him back! But we forget that foundational truth and fall back into law keeping as the way to God.

When we trade legalism for love, we start to see ourselves like God sees us. We come to realize that God loves us with all of our imperfections. We're motivated to give our all for the Beloved!

CHAPTER FOUR

"Grace is the overflowing favor of God,
and you can always count on it being available
to draw upon as needed."
−Oswald Chambers

MULLIGANS

I'll never forget my third game of golf. I'd only played a couple of times, and I was terrible. But my game reached new lows when I played the third time. I stepped up to the first tee, squared my shoulders, and prepared to strike the ball. I reached back with the club, ready to drive the ball down the fairway, launched a mighty swing … and missed the ball.

Completely.

A total whiff.

Talk about embarrassing! And then I did it again. Finally, on my third try, I managed to actually hit the ball. My playing partner's reaction was incredibly generous.

"Hey, just take a mulligan."

I had no idea what a mulligan was. He explained that in a friendly round of golf, your opponent can re-take a flubbed shot, especially if it's the first shot of the game. The mulligan is golf's application of generous forgiveness. It's a chance to start all over again.

Wouldn't it be amazing if we could start all over and take a mulligan here or there? I don't know about you, but I'd love to have a do-over in certain areas of my life. I hunger for my mistakes to be erased and my sins to be forgiven.

The amazing thing is that God does give us a do-over. No matter how badly we've messed up. No matter how awful things have become. With God, we can always have a new beginning, but not because of anything we can do. Our do-over is given because of what God has done. The initiative always belongs to God when it comes to grace.

We see this in Paul's outburst about grace in Ephesians 1. In the original Greek language, verses 3-14 of Ephesians 1 are one long sentence. Paul doesn't come up for air. He's out of breath as he talks about new beginnings. He can't stop talking about our countless blessings in Christ. In the process, he makes it clear that God's grace positions us for a new start: a do-over.

FLAWLESS IN HIS EYES

Grace gives us a new start because God makes us to be flawless in His eyes. Ephesians 1:4 tell us, "Even before he made the world, God loved us and chose us in Christ to be holy and without fault in his eyes." (NLT)

If you follow golf, you're familiar with the Ryder Cup. The Ryder Cup is a trophy that American and European golfers compete for. The top golfers in America square off against the top golfers in Europe. To be on the Ryder Cup team, a golfer must be chosen. The American captain looks for the most elite golfers he can find and chooses the best among them. The European captain does the same.

God doesn't look for the best for His team. He doesn't make a list of people who are superior to everyone else. He chooses people *who will follow* Him. The "choosing" in Ephesians 1 is not about people's eternal destinies. The "you" repeated throughout the chapter refers to God's chosen and is plural: God's new people, the church.

Paul says, God *chose you* to be holy and blameless. God did not choose us to continue in our sin. God's purpose is to create a people who are conformed to the likeness of Christ. Do you know that the word *holy* means "set apart?" It means to live distinctively. We don't live like the people of our culture; we live like God wants us to live. But holiness is not rules without relationship. It's not going through a checklist or coming to church and getting our ticket punched. It's a relationship with God that makes us want to keep His rules!

When I started dating Holly, I did everything I knew how to win her love. I kept McShan Florist in business for two years. I took her to dinner and the symphony and romantic musicals. I lavished her with love, because more than anything else I wanted a deep relationship with her. I was motivated to live in a way I hadn't lived before. I fell in love, and love produced a change nothing else could have created.

> PRACTICAL STEP: Memorize Romans 8:31-39. Recite it to your spouse and your kids. Ask them to memorize it with you. Then talk about what it means for no one to successfully accuse us.

A NEW START THROUGH FORGIVENESS

God's grace also gives us a new start by granting us forgiveness! "He is so rich in kindness and grace that he purchased our freedom with the blood of his Son and forgave our sins. He has showered his kindness on us, along with all wisdom and understanding." (Ephesians 1:7-8, NLT)

Notice Paul's phrase: "He purchased our freedom." This wording originally referred to the marketplace where slaves were bought and sold. In the first century, some people bought slaves so they could set them free. That process was called redemption. When someone purchased a slave to be set free, that person became redeemed! This same process happened to us. We were slaves of sin. We had no way of escape. But God couldn't stand the thought of our enslavement, so He bought us. He redeemed us. He set us free.

Paul says God redeemed us by grace. He forgave us through the riches of His grace. Do you know what brings salvation? Grace—only the grace of God brings salvation. Write that down, because if we put anything else in that sentence, we will never understand grace.

Many people insert something else in that sentence. They think, Good works bring salvation. Or Bible knowledge brings salvation. Or not doing bad things brings salvation. But the only thing that brings salvation is the grace of God.

God offers us the greatest mulligan of all time. And just like a mulligan in golf, we can't buy one or take one on our own. Grace has to be offered by someone on our behalf. God is the one who offers grace to us. In fact, God not only offers a mulligan, He offers to give us a perfect score because He requires a perfect scorecard for us to join Him in eternity. When we turn in our "scorecard" at the end of our life, if we've miss just one putt in an otherwise perfect life, we tragically miss the cut.

But here's the great news. What if someone lived a perfect life, and that person offered us his personally signed scorecard? All we had to do is attest the card and it's ours. We can turn it in on Judgment Day and be home free. That's what grace is all about. With grace, when we mess up, someone else takes the penalty. The good news is that God sent His Son Jesus to pay the penalty for us because we fall short. God offers us the ultimate mulligan in life.

Grace means God gives you a mulligan. He gives you a second chance. But how can there be second chances when we've messed up so badly? How can God forgive our sins? Does He just ignore them? Does He pretend they don't exist?

The answer is found in a phrase Paul uses in Ephesians. "We have redemption through his **blood**." (Ephesians 1:7, NIV) In other words, forgiveness cost God an immeasurable amount. He paid with the blood of His Son. But why does God want blood as a payment for sin? Sin is an affront to God's holiness. Paul says in Romans 6:23 that the punishment for sin is death. When blood is poured out, it signifies that a life has been given. In the Old Testament, the deaths of animals fulfilled this standard of justice. But in the New Testament, Jesus' blood is the payment for sin. Jesus paid with His blood so that God's justice could be satisfied and so that we could be forgiven!

1 Peter 1:18-19 (NLT), "For you know that God paid a ransom to save you from the empty life you inherited from your ancestors. And it was not paid with mere gold or silver, which lose their value. It was the precious blood of Christ, the sinless, spotless Lamb of God." Grace brings salvation because Jesus paid the price for us. Grace means that God forgives every one of our sins. Period. Past, present, future. All.. But you must be willing to receive the gift of forgiveness.

You might pray, "God, I know I could never achieve a perfect score. I thank You for sending Jesus to live a perfect life. Thank You that when I trust Him, He gives me His perfect record, His perfect scorecard. I'm ready to move in a new direction and to do Your will, not mine."

PRACTICAL STEP: Begin each day with this prayer: "Father, I know I'll struggle with sins today. Some I'm aware of, others may not even be on my radar. Remind me of the truth that as I confess my sins to You, You instantly remove those sins through the blood of Your Son. Help me never to forget the gravity of sin or the enormity of Your grace.

THE GUARANTEE OF THE SPIRIT

Grace also gives us a new start by giving us the Holy Spirit. "The Spirit is God's guarantee that he will give us the inheritance he promised and that he has purchased us to be his own people. He did this so we would praise and glorify him." (Ephesians 1:14, NLT) Circle that word *guarantee*. The original word could be translated several ways. It originally meant a *down payment that served as a guarantee*. But it also meant an *engagement ring*.

PRACTICAL STEP: Read the book of Galatians every day for a month (if you read one chapter per day, you will read Galatians 5 times). Allow the message of grace to penetrate your mind and heart. Remember that salvation is based on **only** the gospel of grace!

When I got ready to propose to my wife Holly, I prearranged dinner in a swank restaurant in downtown Dallas. I'd worked it out so that my proposal was delivered along with the dessert. When the time came, the maître' de brought the menu with the proposal and the engagement ring attached. What was I saying by presenting an engagement ring? I was saying: "I want to marry you, Holly, and I'll never back out on you. I'm here to stay. I'll be with you forever."

God says to us, "I promise you I'll be with you forever. I'm in the process of doing new things in your life. I'm giving you a brand new spiritual DNA through my Holy Spirit. You're not the same person you were before I adopted you. I brought you into My family and gave you a new identity. A new attitude. A new you. I'm doing a new thing, and all the scattered pieces of your life will be brought together. And here's how you'll know I'm keeping my promise. I'm giving you an engagement ring. Actually, I'm giving you a part of Myself. I'll never renege on My promise to be with you."

In the movie *Groundhog Day*, Bill Murray plays the role of Phil Connors. Connors is a TV weatherman who is assigned to cover the annual Groundhog Day event, but he's caught in a time loop. He lives the same day over and over again. He figures every day is destined to be the same.

Some of you are frustrated. You feel like every day is destined to be the same. You want to make resolutions, but you're not sure you can keep them. You want to be different, but you don't know how. Let me tell you about the strongest change agent in the universe: the Holy Spirit! The Holy Spirit will radically change your heart. He will change out your old spiritual hard drive and give you a new hard drive with revolutionary spiritual software. When the Holy Spirit gets hold of your life, He does dramatic new things. He creates a new man or a new woman. He will create a brand new you!

A BRAND NEW WORLD

This brand new you is part of the brand new world God is creating! Paul says that God's purpose is "...to bring all things in heaven and on earth together under one head, even Christ." (Ephesians 1:9-10 NIV)

Right now we see discord in the universe. But in the fullness of time, the discord will be over. The deep hunger of our hearts will finally be fulfilled! Everything in heaven and on the earth will come together. The lion and the lamb will come together. Black people and white people and Latino and Asian and Middle Eastern people will come together. The rich and the poor will come together. All the chaos created by the fall of man will be over! Everything that's disconnected will be connected. Broken communities will be reunited. Broken people will come together. Broken hearts will be healed! The whole cosmos will be renewed and brought together under Christ! But this renewal and rebirth all starts in the invisible world. It starts in the unseen world.

God is working to put **you** back together. He wants to do that by giving you a fresh start. He wants to give you a mulligan. Are you looking for a do-over? In golf, it's called a mulligan. In life, it's called a fresh start. A new beginning seems too good to be true. It seems like we should strive to achieve it.

But all we really have to do is receive it.

PRACTICAL STEP: Study the Old Testament names for God, with a view to what each means in terms of God's provision for you. Jehovah Tsidkenu—God is my righteousness. Jehovah Rophe—God is my healer. Jehovah Shammah—God is present. Jehovah Nissi—God is my victory. Jehovah M'kaddesh—God is the One who sanctifies. What do these names mean to you personally?

PART TWO

GRACE: GOD'S GREATEST CHALLENGE

CHAPTER FIVE

"We need to remember that we are saved by grace when we fail.
But we need to remember it much more when we succeed."
–Timothy Keller

DILEMMAS

Grace is the free gift of God. When I describe grace to unbelievers, they sometimes instinctively react against it. "How could God just forgive, with no strings attached?" they reason. But their reasoning betrays a misunderstanding of grace. Grace costs something. In fact, its price is incalculable. The Bible explains that grace is made possible because of the cross of Christ.

One of the most popular sites in Jerusalem is Golgotha. The Gospel writers call the place where Jesus was crucified *Golgotha*—an Aramaic word that means "the skull." The Latin form of the word is *Calvary*. Scripture doesn't reveal the exact location of Golgotha. It just says that Jesus' crucifixion took place *outside* the city of Jerusalem. Jewish law did not permit executions and burials inside the city. We also know that Jesus was crucified near a well-traveled road, since people who passed by mocked him. The Romans chose conspicuous places by major highways for their public executions. The crucifixion probably took place on a hill, because it was visible at a distance. But no matter where Golgotha is located, it is the site of the most important event in human history.

But what does the cross really mean? We know when Jesus died and how He died—but the bigger question is, *why* did He die? The Bible's answer is that Christ took responsibility for your sins—there was no other way to secure salvation. But what evidence is there that Christ became your substitute?

THE TRIAL OF JESUS

One of the most powerful proofs that Christ became your substitute is the trial of Jesus. Jesus suffered the greatest miscarriage of justice the world has ever seen. He was the only perfect man who ever lived—but He was treated more savagely than anyone has ever been treated. Matthew 26 tells about Jesus' trial before the Sanhedrin, the supreme court of the Jews. The chief priests had searched for false evidence against Jesus so they could put Him to death. They accuse Him of blasphemy and pronounce Him worthy of death. They spit in His face and strike Him with their fists. They slap Him and say, "Prophesy to us, Messiah. Who hit you?"

Jesus' trial is a kangaroo court. But the travesty continues when the Jewish leaders drag Jesus to Pilate. The Jewish leaders want Jesus dead. The big guns of the Jewish religion are furious over Jesus' popularity. But they don't have the legal authority to order an execution. Only a Roman court can do that. So they haul Jesus in front of Pilate, the Roman governor. Notice three things about Jesus and His trial before Pilate.

JESUS WAS SILENT SO HE COULD
BE YOUR SPOKESMAN

Matthew 27:11-14 (NIV) says, "Meanwhile Jesus stood before the governor, and the governor asked him, 'Are you the king of the Jews?'" 'Yes, it is as you say,' Jesus answered. When he was accused by the chief priests and the elders, he gave no answer. Then Pilate asked him, 'Don't you hear the testimony they are bringing against you?' But Jesus made no reply, not even to a single charge—to the great amazement of the governor."

Pilate was governor from AD 26 to AD 36. He ruled over Judea on behalf of Rome. Pilate had life-or-death authority over accused criminals. The Jewish leaders knew they didn't have authority to murder Jesus. They needed a charge that would hold up in a civil court. Their best shot was to accuse Jesus of claiming to be the king of the Jews; it sounded like treason. They argued that Jesus was a traitor who had stirred up the people against Rome. None of that was true, of course. But the Jewish supreme court filed charges of treason against Jesus because Jesus was disloyal to Caesar. It was a silly charge: everybody knew the Jews themselves hated Caesar. But they were desperate to find some charge to bring against Christ. So they accused Jesus of being a terrorist who was undermining Rome.

Pilate kicked off the interrogation with a question: "Are you the king of the Jews?" In other words, how do you respond to the charge against you? And Jesus said, "Yes, it is as you say" But then Pilate is blown out of his chair by what happens next. Matthew states that when the chief priests and elders accuse Jesus, He gave no answer. Jesus stood in silence.

So why didn't Jesus offer a defense? He kept silent then so he could speak on our behalf now! He didn't offer any earthly defense, so that he could defend us against the charges we face before a righteous God!

Revelation 12 says that Satan is the great accuser. Rev. 12:10 (NIV) states, "Then I heard a loud voice in heaven say: 'Now have come the salvation and the power and the kingdom of our God, and the authority of his Messiah. For the accuser of our brothers and sisters, who accuses them before our God day and night, has been hurled down." Satan stands in the courtroom pointing his bony finger of accusation at us, indicting us for our sins. But none of his charges will stick because Jesus was willing to remain silent.

Romans 8:33-34 (NLT) states, "Who dares accuse us whom God has chosen for his own? No one—for God himself has given us right standing with himself. Who then will condemn us? No one—for Christ Jesus died for us and was raised to life for us, and he is sitting in the place of honor at God's right hand, pleading for us."

So if you're in Christ, you don't have to worry about what will happen when you stand before God at the end of time. Jesus pleads for you. He intercedes for you. He declares you not guilty! He was silent so He could become your spokesman!

JESUS WAS CONDEMNED SO
YOU COULD BE CLEARED

Pilate comes up with what seems like an ingenious plan. He offers the crowd a choice between Jesus and Barabbas. (See Matthew 27:15-25) Pilate is actually trying to get off the hook in a last-ditch effort to get out of this mess. He knows there's no real case against Jesus. In the middle of all this chaos, Pilate has a chance to do the right thing. While he is sitting on the judge's bench, he receives a message from his wife. Mrs. Pilate has had a dream. The dream inspires her to send Pilate this message: "Don't have anything to do with that innocent man. I've suffered a nightmare because of Him."

The warning only increased the pressure on Pilate. God used a dream to warn him not to kill Jesus, but Pilate still wouldn't listen. Pilate surrendered to the demand of the crowd: "Crucify him!" He tried to exonerate himself. He took a bowl of water and started washing his hands, saying, "I am innocent of this man's blood. It is your responsibility."

But then comes one of the most shocking statements in scripture. The people respond, "Let His blood be on us and on our children." Imagine asking for your children to bear the guilt for crucifying the Son of God! It's true that this crowd bore guilt for their sins. But it wasn't the Jews alone. Acts 4:27 says that Herod was guilty, Pilate was guilty, the Gentiles were guilty, and the people of Israel were guilty. There was plenty of blame to spread around.

WERE YOU THERE?

One truth about Jesus' death is truly convicting: **I am guilty**. And you are guilty.

PRACTICAL SECRET: Memorize Bible verses that emphasize that Christianity is not spelled d-o, but d-o-n-e. For example: Titus 3:5, "He saved us, not because of righteous things we have done, but because of His mercy."

It's easy to condemn Pilate and miss our own guilt. We all have blood on our hands. We all share guilt in the murder of Christ. We're all culpable! You might ask how this could be true. We were there because each of us played a part. We were all there, not just as spectators, but as participants. Our sins put Him there.

We are the reason Jesus went to the cross. Before we can see the cross as something done *for* us, we have to realize it was something done *by* us! 1 Peter 2:24 (NIV) tells us, "He himself bore our sins in his body on the tree, so that we might die to sins and live for righteousness; by his wounds you have been healed." Our sins nailed Jesus to the cross. That's the bad news.

But here's the good news. Jesus died so that we would not be condemned! Let's say you haven't had a quiet time for three weeks. You think to yourself, *I'm not a very good Christian. I'm busy at home. I'm busy at work. I'm just trying to survive. I never have time for the Bible. I haven't had time to really pray. I'm not a very good Christian.* Aren't you really saying that since you failed to have a quiet time, you stand condemned before God? That your relationship with God is destroyed if you go through a season where your quiet time with God is inconsistent? But here's the reality: God's grace extended to you in Christ didn't go away for three weeks when you stopped having quiet time. It was still there.

Or maybe the reason you don't feel like a very good Christian is because you fell into sin, which leaves you thinking, *I can't believe I did this. This was the sin I told God I wasn't going to do again. I swore this off. I thought I was done with this, and now I did it again. I hate myself. I'm not a very good Christian.* But the cross says that you're forgiven if you confess your sins and come to God with a penitent heart. 1 John 1:9 (RSV) assures us that "If we confess our sins, he is faithful and just to forgive our sins, and to cleanse us from all unrighteousness." Jesus died for your *slimy sins.* Jesus died for your repeated sins. When you don't feel like a very good Christian because of these sins, confess your sins to God. Come to God with a heart that's broken over your sins. Ask for His forgiveness!

Christ assumed the guilt of our sins. Christ was convicted of crimes He never committed. The sinless one was made to be sin. He took our curse, so we could receive His blessing. Jesus was condemned, so that you could be set free! You were condemned, but now you walk out a free man. But how is that possible? How can people who deserve condemnation be released? How can God grant us freedom without compromising His perfection?

JESUS WAS TORTURED SO GOD
COULD BE VINDICATED

But did Jesus really have to go through all of this? He did, for two reasons. He had to pay the price for our sins. He had to become our substitute. But there's another reason we often overlook: He had to satisfy the just requirements of a holy God. Most people don't lose sleep over how God can be just and loving to sinners at the same time.

We tend to point the finger at God and say, "How can you punish sinners? How can you let people go to hell?" But the Bible asks a different question: "God, how can You be just and still let rebels into heaven?"

We have to realize that God's forgiveness of our sins is a threat to His character. Carnegie Simpson said, "Forgiveness is for God the profoundest of problems."[7] We think of forgiveness as something that's fairly simple. But God was presented with a severe dilemma. He couldn't look past sin or let bygones be bygones. God knew that sin had to be dealt with.

Who did Jesus die for? He died for sinners. He died for you and me. But ultimately, Jesus died for God. Watchman Nee said, "If I would appreciate the blood of Christ I must accept God's valuation of it, for the blood is not primarily for me but for God." We think of the gospel as the answer to our problem, and in many ways it is. But first of all, it is God's answer to a divine problem. The cross was absolutely necessary to God's vindication and the declaration of his glory. It was crucial for demonstrating his justice and his righteousness!

How is it that a righteous judge can declare guilty people to be not guilty? God faced a challenge. He chose to let the sins of humanity accumulate up until the time of Christ. It isn't that He was ignoring wrong. But out of His personal forbearance, He'd patiently endured man's sins. But then God presented Christ as a sacrifice of atonement. Why? To demonstrate His justice! God had shown amazing restraint. But He couldn't let this backlog of sins mount up indefinitely. If God chose to ignore sin, He would violate His divine character as the righteous judge of the universe. So in Christ, God announced the sentence against sin: He condemned our sins in Christ.

A GOD OF MERCY AND JUSTICE

The cross is a dramatic demonstration of the justice and mercy of God. If God had forgiven sin but never punished wrong, He would be a God of mercy but not a God of justice. If He had punished wrong but refused to forgive, He would be a God of justice but not a God of mercy. The cross is where justice and mercy come together in an amazing paradox! How are we declared not guilty? Not because God waved a magic wand and announced it. It was because God Himself in the person of Christ guaranteed that the demands of justice were met!

PRACTICAL STEP: Imagine that you were the only person on planet Earth when Christ came. Imagine that He chose to die for you, only you. Then celebrate the value of your soul through the perspective of a loving Savior.

Steve Winger tells about a student in a college logic class. The professor told the students, "You can bring to the final exam as much information as you can fit on a piece of paper, 8.5 by 11 inches." You know what the students did: they copied copious notes scribbled on their crib sheets. But one student was brighter. He brought a blank piece of paper, put it down on the floor next to the desk, and invited an advanced logic student to stand on the piece of paper. Then he asked the logic guru all the answers he needed for the test. He was the only student in the class to make an A.

When I stand before God at the end of time, if He should ask me, "Art, why should I let you into heaven?" I will point to the person standing next to me, Jesus Christ, and I will say, "I don't have any reason for you to permit me into heaven. But the one standing next to me has met all requirements for my admission."

CHAPTER SIX

"The meaning of life. The wasted years of life.
The poor choices of life.
God answers the mess of life with one word: 'grace.'"
–Max Lucado

DIS-GRACED

We're familiar with phrases related to shame. "Ain't that a shame?" "That's a crying shame." "Fool me once, shame on you, fool me twice, shame on me." "The walk of shame." "The cone of shame." "Shame on you."

What's the difference between shame and pity? Someone joked, "If a busload of lawyers goes over a cliff, and there are no survivors, that's known as a pity. If there were any empty seats, that's a shame."

It's critical that we know how to process shame in a healthy way. If not, we will take actions to compensate for the shame—actions that may complicate our lives and compound our problems. There are three primary sources of shame in our lives.

SHAME BECAUSE OF SIN

Adam and Eve were ashamed because of their sin. They tried to hide from God because they didn't want their sin to be exposed. Shame can be a good thing. When shame results from true guilt in our lives, it's an indicator light that something is wrong, that we need to correct something. This might be called legitimate shame. Legitimate shame creates pain in our hearts that makes us sensitive to sin. Without this pain we wouldn't feel the motivation to honor God. We'd be like a leper who doesn't feel pain. Jeremiah 8:12 (NIV) states, "Are they ashamed of their detestable conduct? No, they have no shame at all; they do not even know how to blush ..."

There is a difference between legitimate shame and illegitimate shame. If you know you should treat people with patience but you frequently lose your temper, you should feel shame. But if you have four preschoolers at home and you feel bad because your house is not spotless, you're experiencing false shame, illegitimate shame. You're trying to live up to an artificial standard.

PRACTICAL STEP: With a close friend or a Christian counselor, discuss an event or experience in your life that has caused you great shame. Then ask the friend or counselor to pray God's blessing over you, that you will be able to jettison the shame through the power of Christ.

SHAME BECAUSE OF SHORTCOMINGS

Some feelings of shame are not caused by sin, but because of shortcomings. We might call this "misplaced shame." There's an example of this from the 2017 NCAA basketball tournament, March Madness. Vanderbilt was playing Northwestern. Vanderbilt took a one-point lead with 17 seconds to go in the game. But Vanderbilt guard Matthew Fisher-Davis fouled a Northwestern player. The Northwestern player went to the free throw line and sank both free throws. This gave Northwestern the victory, and they moved on to the next round.

Fisher-Davis made a big mistake. He lost track of the score. It was devastating for him. Maybe you dropped the ball in the big game. Or you didn't meet your sales quota. Or didn't achieve the score you wanted on the test. This is what we call misplaced shame, shame that has nothing to do with sin, but a feeling of failure because of our shortcomings.

SHAME BECAUSE OF IGNORANCE

Shame because of our ignorance is another subset of misplaced shame. I went hunting years ago with some buddies. I was a rookie and had never fired a gun. My friends gave me a quick lesson in firing a rifle, but we went the entire weekend without spotting a single deer. A year later we went hunting again. I climbed up into the blind and waited. About dusk a big buck sauntered up. I was excited but completely forgot the previous year's shooting lesson. I lifted the rifle but failed to position the butt of the gun against my shoulder. I took aim and fired (and missed the buck, by the way). The gun went off, and the scope of the rifle jammed into my forehead. Blood spewed from my crescent-shaped wound. I slunk back to the cabin to face my seasoned hunter friends. As soon as I walked in, they started laughing and pointing. They knew exactly what had happened. "Scope cut," they shouted! They were laughing because I hadn't known what I was doing! I experienced shame because of my ignorance!

PRACTICAL STEP: Ask God to help you distinguish between what you have done and who you are. Ask Him to replace any illegitimate shame you may feel with the peace of the Holy Spirit.

SHAME PRODUCES EMOTIONAL PAIN

No matter the source of your shame, it can lead to emotional problems. Emotional pain can be so real that it can cause physical pain. In the pain of anger, shame looks for someone to blame. You might blame yourself for failing to reach your expectations. You might blame other people for criticizing you. You might blame God for struggles in your life. In the pain of anxiety, you think about a past failure that makes you anxious that you might fail again. In the pain of depression, shame convinces you there's no cure for your situation and your life will never be good again. Shame can lead to hopelessness and despair. Shamed people often try to medicate their pain to deaden it, which only makes things worse.

Many phrases describe our feelings of shame.

Damaged Goods. Years ago, a friend of mine developed an addiction to marijuana. He said that his shame made him feel like "damaged goods." Damaged goods have been dropped, chipped, soiled, or ruined. Maybe you've been divorced. Maybe you've been adopted or had an abortion. Maybe you lost a job you thought was your life's calling. Or maybe you've been sexually abused. Life events can leave you feeling like damaged goods.

Disgust. The deep emotional response to shame is disgust. Lewis Smedes refers to it as feeling "like a hunk of lead in our hearts ... like an invisible load that weighs our spirits down and crushes out our joy. It is a lingering sorrow."[8] You hate yourself for falling short of your expectations or for letting others down.

Brene Brown quotes a number of people who described how shame felt to them: "Shame is getting laid off and having to tell my pregnant wife. Shame is having someone ask me, 'When are you due?' when I'm not pregnant. Shame is hiding the fact that I'm in recovery. Shame is raging at my kids. Shame is bankruptcy. Shame is my boss calling me an idiot in front of the client. Shame is not making partner. Shame is my husband leaving me for my next-door neighbor. Shame is my wife asking me for a divorce and telling me that she wants children, but not with me. Shame is my DUI. Shame is infertility. Shame is telling my fiancé that my dad lives in France when in fact he's in prison. Shame is Internet porn. Shame is flunking out of school. Twice. Shame is hearing my parents fight through the walls and wondering if I'm the only one who feels this afraid."[9]

Exposed. Shamed people live with a fear of being exposed. They think if other people really knew them, they wouldn't have anything to do with them. That's the way a lot of people feel about church. "They wouldn't want me here." Fear of exposure is central to the idea of shame.

Flawed. Some people have described their shame as feeling flawed and defective, like there's something wrong with them. The truth is, there IS something wrong ... with all of us. But there's a distinction between legitimate shame and misplaced shame. In the case of legitimate shame, we've all missed the target of God's perfection. This is where we have to hear the message of grace. The gospel is knowing that you are far worse than you ever dared imagine, and knowing you are far more loved than you ever dreamed. We don't go wrong by believing we are flawed; we go wrong by taking the giant leap of logic that because we are flawed, we are worthless. We are beyond hope and even God can't help us. This is when we start to unravel.

PRACTICAL STEP: You may need a recovery group of some kind to help you process and pray through your sense of shame. Discover the power of community by sharing your shame with the group.

THE ANSWER TO OUR SHAME

So what is the answer to our sense of shame, whether that shame comes from sin or shortcomings or ignorance? The answer is the cross and seeing the shame that Jesus experienced for you and me. When we hear the cry of the cross, we find an answer for our shame.

The cross was more than a cross of pain. It was a cross of shame. The cross was the ultimate symbol of shame. Hebrews 12:2 (NIV) says, "...fixing our eyes on Jesus, the pioneer and perfecter of faith. For the joy set before him he endured the cross, *scorning its shame*, and sat down at the right hand of the throne of God." Christ was willing to endure the shame of the cross so He could secure our salvation. The cross was the basement of human debasement!

A Danish newspaper poked fun at Muhammad with 12 cartoons. Muslims revolted. They burned flags, torched embassies, and stoned at least one Christian church. The cartoonists went into hiding in fear for their lives. Why did Muslims react so violently? Because they couldn't stomach the idea of an insulted Savior, a God covered in shame.

It's fascinating that most Muslims have been taught that Jesus was not crucified. Muslims believe that Allah saved the Messiah from the shame of crucifixion. This is the most fundamental difference between Christ and Muhammad and between a Muslim and a Christian. Muslims can't imagine a Messiah who would tolerate suffering and shame. In contrast, our Savior took our shame upon Himself because of His great love for us.

THE CROSS WAS ASININE

Choosing the cross as the symbol of faith was literally considered asinine. We see evidence of this in graffiti from the second century found on the wall of a house in Rome. The graffiti pictures a caricature of a crucifixion. A crude drawing of a man stretched out on a cross bears the head of a donkey. To the left stands a second man, with one arm raised in worship. Scribbled underneath are the words ALEXAMENOS CEBETE THEON: Alexamenos worships God. This graphic cartoon is displayed in a museum in Rome. The artist's message is clear: Christians worship a donkey, an ass. The artist lampoons the idea of a god on a cross.

As horrific as physical suffering was for Jesus, His psychological suffering was far worse. It's striking that when Matthew recounts the crucifixion, he doesn't pause over the grisly details of the hammer being driven into the hands and feet. He zeroes in on the shame of the cross. Victims of crucifixion were usually made to wear a placard around their neck. The Romans would write on the placard the crime the person was condemned for to emphasize the shame was inflicted on victims of crucifixion. So why this focus on insults and derision? Because a major component of Jesus' pain on the cross was the shame He bore—not only the shame inflicted that day, but the crushing shame experienced by every human who ever lived.

Maybe you know what it's like to suffer shame, to be humiliated. Maybe you have been insulted and scorned. Perhaps you were sexually abused, and you live with the shame of those memories every day. Maybe you were verbally abused and mocked. Let me encourage you to remember that Jesus was treated with shame and contempt. He was taunted and jeered, insulted and vilified. During His life on earth Jesus was called a bastard, a drunkard, and a devil. But the most crushing weight of Jesus' shame came in the moments He hung on the cross and carried the full weight of the shame of the world—of every pervert, murderer, thief, drug lord, debased and debauched human who ever lived.

The cross is the answer for our shame because it reminds us that no matter how horribly we've been treated, we have a Savior who understands our shame and who took our shame on Himself. If Christ had not been insulted, there would be no salvation. We wouldn't have a rescue from our shame!

Jesus was shamed so you and I wouldn't have to be. Jesus was treated as worthless. Damaged goods. Defective and no good. But when Jesus went to the cross, He established your worth once and for all. Even though you and I are flawed, we are not worthless. We are of infinite value: broken vessels, but priceless vessels.

CHAPTER SEVEN

*"Those who look to him are radiant; their faces
are never covered with shame."*
–Psalm 34:5 (NIV)

UNASHAMED

The cross announces the difference between religion and Christianity. Religion is a set of beliefs. Christianity is God hanging on a cross. Sometimes churches offer a class called "Why Did Jesus Have to Die?" But this isn't the right question. The more appropriate question is, "Why was Jesus *crucified*?" Crucifixion is a singular kind of death. It was reserved for slaves and criminals. The Jews considered anyone who was crucified to be condemned by God. "Cursed is everyone who is hung on a pole." (Galatians 3:13) NIV Crucifixion was the ultimate statement that a victim was rejected and forsaken by God. No one expected a crucified Messiah.

The cross was designed to create the greatest possible shame for the victim. Suffering is one thing, but suffering that degrades is another. Crucifixion was the ultimate insult to personal dignity: the most humiliating and dehumanizing death possible. Degradation was the point. Victims were crucified naked at a major crossroads and left to be eaten by birds and beasts. While the cross made it possible for God to give us grace, it was the most *disgraceful* event in history.

Jesus suffered for our shame. He was publicly beaten, mocked, whipped, spat upon, and nailed to the cross. In the Old Testament, spitting in someone's face was a gesture of contempt, a deliberate insult. You might remember that during his trials, Job was such an object of disgrace that people spat upon him in disgust (Job:30:10).. Scripture predicted that Jesus would be spat upon. Isaiah 50:6 (NLT), "I offered my back to those who beat me, my cheeks to those who pulled out my beard; I did not hide my face from mocking and spitting."

Roman soldiers not only covered Jesus with spit, they ridiculed His claim to be a king. They hit Him again and again with a staff. The staff represented a scepter and was intended to lampoon His claim to be king. They feigned the kind of veneration shown to royalty. Isaiah 53:5-7 (NIV) says, "He was oppressed and afflicted, yet he did not open his mouth; he was led like a lamb to the slaughter, and as a sheep before its shearers is silent, so he did not open his mouth."

If Christ had never been shamed, He could never be our Savior. Psalm 22:7 says, "All that look upon me have laughed me to scorn; they have spoken with their lips and have wagged their heads." Mohammed lived to be honored: Christ lived to be insulted. The cross was ignominious. The cross was insulting. Enduring mockery was the essence of Jesus' mission. Isaiah 52:14 (NLT) states, "But many were amazed when they saw him. His face was so disfigured he seemed hardly human, and from his appearance, one would scarcely know he was a man." Psalm 69:19 (NIV) says, "You know how I am scorned, disgraced and shamed; all my enemies are before you."

The cross is singular in its shame because of Jesus' cry of forsakenness. Jesus' cry rings out from the cross: "My God, my God, why have you forsaken me." These words set the cross apart from every other death. The cross was unique because in that moment, the Father placed the sins of the world on Jesus. Who was then treated as if He had committed every sin that had ever been committed or would be committed.

2 Corinthians 5:21 (NIV) tells us, "For God made him who had no sin to be sin for us, so that in Him we might become the righteousness of God." Many have been executed. Many have been hanged. Some have even been crucified. But because of the cry of forsakenness, the cross represents something unique. No greater pain has ever been experienced than the hell Christ suffered in this moment. He was punished for every sin ever committed in history. He bore our sin and shame and was forsaken and punished so we could be reconciled to God.

"My God, my God, why have you forsaken me?" This wasn't a rhetorical question. The answer was and is: For you, for me, for the world. Jesus was forsaken by God so we would never have to be. The judgment that should have fallen on us fell on Jesus in our stead.

PROCESSING SHAME

Shame is related to a wrong-doing. Our culture says that all shame is bad and wrong and unhealthy. But this is not true according to the Bible. Some experiences of shame are healthy, but it's not our role to put shame on other people. There is shame we feel on our own when we've done something wrong. Shame also alerts us that a relationship is in jeopardy because of wrongdoing on our part. Shame is designed to help us tap the brakes when we're responsible for wrong behavior. Legitimate shame is not the end of the world. However, it is the end of the world if we've lost the capacity to feel shame. 2 Peter 2:2 tells us, "Many will follow their evil teaching and shameful immorality. And because of these teachers, the way of truth will be slandered."

WHAT DO WE DO WITH
LEGITIMATE SHAME?

When we experience legitimate shame, we should look to the cross and remember that Christ took our shame so that we wouldn't have to. Amir is the protagonist in the novel *The Kite Runner*. Amir's life takes a dramatic turn when he fails to rush to the aid of friend, Hassan. Hassan is raped by the bully Assef. Amir stands behind the fence and watches it happen. He pretends not to know about it. "I became what I am today at the age of twelve, on a frigid overcast day in the winter of 1975. I remember the precise moment, crouching behind a crumbling mud wall, peeking into the alley near the frozen creek. That was a long time ago, but it's wrong what they say about the past, I've learned, about how you can bury it. Because the past claws its way out. Looking back now, I realize I have been peeking into that deserted alley for the last twenty-six years."[10]

That's what shame will do to us unless we go to the cross. Shame will haunt us and intimidate us unless we give it to God, and ask for forgiveness. 1 Peter 2:6 (NIV) says, "See, I lay a stone in Zion, a chosen and precious cornerstone, and the one who trusts in him will never be put to shame." Legitimate shame calls attention to what we've done, not who we are. When Satan calls us, he calls us by our sin. But when Jesus calls us, He calls us by our name. We are more than our sin and more than our shame.

WHAT DO WE DO WITH MISPLACED SHAME?

There is shame we feel that we shouldn't feel, but we do. We feel this shame when we feel out of place and as if we don't belong. We also feel it when people shame each other when they shouldn't.

Proverbs 29:25 (NIV) says, "The fear of human opinion disables; trusting in GOD protects you from that."

Galatians 1:10 (NLT) states, "Obviously, I'm (Paul) not trying to win the approval of people, but of God. If pleasing people were my goal, I would not be Christ's servant." Misplaced shame often results when we compare ourselves to others. We're continually comparing ourselves to others—people's airbrushed images or highlight reels on their Facebook feeds.

PRACTICAL STEP: Write down any experience or action you are ashamed of. Then, take the piece of paper and burn it, remembering that God doesn't want you to hold onto your sense of shame.

When we soak in shame, we need to revisit the cross and recall the words of the great song "How Deep the Father's Love for Us": "How deep the Father's love for us, How vast beyond all measure, That He should give His only Son, To make a wretch His treasure, How great the pain of searing loss, The Father turns His face away, As wounds which mar the chosen One, Bring many sons to glory Behold the Man upon a cross, My sin upon His shoulders, Ashamed I hear my mocking voice, Call out among the scoffers. It was my sin that held Him there, Until it was accomplished His dying breath has brought me life, I know that it is finished."

CHAPTER EIGHT

"It is grace at the beginning, and grace at the end.
So that when you and I come to lie upon our death beds,
the one thing that should comfort and help and strengthen us there
is the thing that helped us in the beginning.
Not what we have been, not what we have done,
but the Grace of God in Jesus Christ our Lord."
–Martyn Lloyd-Jones

TWO WORDS

One of the most poignant cries in the world is the cry for forgiveness. Guilt cries out for an answer. Some people cry out for forgiveness but don't think it's possible.

"I'm too guilty."

"I'm too broken."

"It's too late."

We assume that forgiveness is impossible. Some of you are there. You've made such a mess of things you figure there's no way you could have a relationship with God. Some people feel locked into their regrets about the past. A website called *"Secret Regrets"* lists thousands of posts from people expressing regret for something they did. Here are some excerpts:

> "I regret when you were a baby and I was eighteen that my boyfriend was violent and I was too scared to stand up for you and me and they took you away. That was twenty years ago and I think about you every day."

"I regret watching pornography for the last 16 years of my life. Even if it was an occasional, four times a month habit, it still destroyed my sense of beauty, purity, and respect for the opposite sex."

"I regret cheating on my husband and carrying on an affair for nearly 2 months. I regret not telling him my thoughts before I acted on them because we could have talked through my feelings without causing any real hurt. I wonder if I will always feel guilty and if he will always feel hurt."

"I regret sleeping with this girl in my church. She loved me so much but I couldn't return that love. I regret being unfaithful to God and I regret playing with her feelings."

"I regret ruining my relationship with my parents over a boy. I regret ever letting it go as far as it did where I was constantly lying and feeling the deep sorrow of regret in my stomach every time I would lie straight to their face to cover up hanging out with him.

"It's been months now since any trouble has happened and I still feel the guilt. I feel the guilt still now even though I am no longer lying."

"Having so many regrets in my life has caused me so much pain and suffering. Making a stupid mistake once and then other stupid mistakes over and over all culminated into a complete breakdown. Reading other posts and realizing that this depression/shame/guilt could go on forever is crippling."[11]

How would you fill in the blank? "I regret _____."

Make two columns:

BEFORE   AFTER

Write down your condition before you chose to follow Christ. Then write down your condition after you chose to follow Christ.

We may assume that what we've done is unforgivable. Guilt and shame are our constant companions. We can't forgive ourselves, and we figure that God never would, either. Negative emotions eat at us. Remorse over a poor choice. Shame about the marriage that didn't work, the habit we couldn't quit, the temptation we didn't resist, or the courage we couldn't find.

What is the answer? We long to be set free from guilt and shame and regret. The answer is found in two words that occur again and again in scripture. Every time these two words appear, they announce something new. Something dramatic. Something life-changing. Something completely different will transform man's relationship with God. These two words declare that no failure is final and no regret must last forever.

And what are they?

"But now." But—a conjunction that tells us the *converse* or the opposite of what was before is true. When? Now. We were unforgiven, but *now* we're forgiven. We were lost, but *now* we're found. We were riddled with regret, but *now* we live with freedom and joy. Notice carefully:

BUT NOW!

Ephesians 2:13 (NLT) declares, "Once you were far away from God, **but now** you have been brought near to him through the blood of Christ." 1 Peter 2:10 (NIV) reassures us, "Once you were not a people, **but now** you are the people of God; once you had not received mercy, **but now** you have received mercy."

1 Peter 2:25 (NIV) states, "For you were like sheep going astray, **but now** you have returned to the Shepherd and Overseer of your souls."

All of these point to *a new time* in history. *A new way* of relating to God. *A new opportunity* that we have because of Jesus! Something brand new, something unheard of. Perhaps the most significant "but now" in the Bible is found in Romans 3:21 (NLT): "**But now** God has shown us a way to be made right with him without keeping the requirements of the law, as was promised in the writings of Moses and the prophets long ago. We are made right with God by placing our faith in Jesus Christ."

A DISMAL PICTURE

Paul paints a dismal picture of man's condition. Lost. Hopeless. Condemned because of God's wrath against sin (Romans 1:18). Given over to sinful desires (Romans 1:24). Filled with every kind of wickedness (Romans 1:29). Man is without excuse, storing up wrath against himself for the day of God's wrath (Romans 2:5). The Jews were lost because even though they knew the law of God, and they didn't keep the law of God. The Gentiles were lost because they knew there was a God, but they refused His ways. Jews and Gentiles were both under the power of sin, Romans 3:9.

No one is righteous. No one can measure up to God's perfect standards. The result? Everyone stands condemned before a holy God. We often think we're righteous because we think we're better than other people. We like to point out that we're superior to other people who've sinned more than we have. But the standard of measurement for righteousness isn't people: it's a perfect and holy God. Isaiah 64:6 says that all our righteousness is like filthy rags. Romans 3:10 says there's no one righteous, not even one. Our condition was hopeless. We were staring eternal death in the face, and there was no way out.

But this is where we come to the two words that revolutionize our relationship with God. Romans 3:21 (NLT) announces, "**But now** God has shown us a way to be made right with him without keeping the requirements of the law ..." Circle those words. Underline them. Highlight them.

But now. In the past I was condemned, *but now* I'm not condemned. Then I was a dead man walking, *but now* I am alive in Christ. In the next chapter, we'll explore the massive impact of these two words.

CHAPTER NINE

"Amazing Grace, how sweet the sound, that saved a wretch like me.
*I once was lost, **but now** I'm found, was blind, but now I see."*
—John Newton

METAPHORS

The movement to "But now" is described in the Bible by three powerful metaphors.

A METAPHOR FROM THE LAW COURT

We were condemned to die in God's court of law, *but now* we are justified! Paul says that in His gracious kindness, God *declared us not guilty*! Picture yourself standing before a judge in a courtroom. You are under sentence of death because you have violated the law. You are condemned to die on death row, with no hope of pardon. You are sentenced without the possibility of appeal. All that awaits you is the fulfillment of your sentence.

"But now"...the gospel changes everything. God, the Judge Himself intervenes. He grants full pardon and you stand before Him without condemnation. The law clearly holds you guilty. The law has a purpose. But the law cannot save you. God's grace alone can save you. Your right standing before the law is the result of His pardon, His free gift.

You have been given the opportunity to walk from the courtroom a free man or woman—an unfathomable gift—based upon your faith in the Judge's pardon. In the same way, our right standing with God comes through faith Jesus Christ's substitutionary death for us!

The letters BC refer to a historical moment in time. BC refers to history "before Christ." But more than history is divided by those letters. Your personal history is divided by those letters! There's a BC in my life. Before Christ, I was hopelessly lost and condemned by God. Before Christ, I was sentenced to hell, "but now" things are different!

One of the striking things in the verses in Romans 3 and others above is that they are objective. In other words, Paul doesn't talk about how we feel—he talks about *who we are*. God's statement of who we are is not subjective. When we put our faith in Christ, God makes us right with Himself—not because of how we feel but because of who He makes us. Our new identity in Him is His gift. It's easy to forget this.

It's easy to think our relationship with God is based on performance when we feel good about our behavior. At these times we tend to think positively about our relationship with God. But later we may wonder if God still loves us when we do something self-centered, like acting out of pride by trying to look important—and then feeling like an idiot.

We may wake up feeling good about our relationship with God. But then we pass by the swimsuit edition of Sports Illustrated and linger as we look. Later we realize how rebellious against God we were in that moment. In those moments, we feel horrible about ourselves and wonder if God still loves us.

I may feel good about my relationship with God until I twist the truth and justify it as a little white lie. Later I recognize my sin and I wonder if God still loves me.

Maybe you know what it's like to hear voices of condemnation.

"You aren't good enough."

"You'll never improve."

"You failed—again."

"God doesn't love you."

Where do voices like these come from?

They come from Satan. Satan constantly accuses. Revelation 12:10 identifies Satan as "the one who accused our brothers and sisters before our God day and night." Satan never shuts up. He's constantly whispering in our ear, accusing us of this, and accusing us of that. Indicting us. Beating us up. Sowing seeds of doubt about our relationship with God. Dredging up our past. Relentlessly working to convince us that God doesn't love us. Trying to persuade us that our sins have condemned us.

This is the kind of thinking we struggle with when we forget "but now." "But now" says that our relationship with God doesn't depend on our getting things right; "but now" rests in faith that Jesus got it right. "But now" is not about our feelings; "but now" is about the fact of the crucifixion and salvation.

"But now" says it's not about we measuring up, it's about Christ measuring up. We're not declared right one moment and then declared not right the next.

"But now" says that our relationship with Christ is not about our performance. How do we prove ourselves good enough in the work world? When we want a job, we send in a resumé. We point to our performance. We list all the things that we think qualify us for the job—everything we can think of that might qualify us.

We think the same thing is true about religion, that religion is about performance. We get out our performance record, and if it's good enough, then we qualify before God. Then Paul comes along and says, for the first time in history there's a different approach. Someone earned a perfect record: Christ. When we put our trust in what Christ has done, we receive His perfect record! This unmerited grace is the opposite of religion.

We think of The Law of Moses and The Ten Commandments with a capital L. But the law is about more than that. David Zahl states, "Little-l law is the air we breathe as human beings, the default setting, the quid pro quo that characterizes our internal life. Here's the logic: to get approval, you have to achieve. Behavior precedes belovedness. Climb the ladder, or else ... The woman on the street may not have given the fifth chapter of Matthew's gospel a second thought since Sunday school, yet she is likely on intimate terms with the condemning echoes issuing from Madison Avenue ("Thou shalt be skinny, successful, independent, and self-actualized.")" She has that feeling of never being quite enough, which drives her striving and exhaustion. This drives our busyness. In our culture, busyness is more than a description of how we're doing. It's an indicator of our worth."[12]

There's something about the law that we love. It puts us in the driver's seat. If we can just do x, y, or z, then we will get the result we want. If we can just be a certain kind of person or project certain qualities, then we will be loved. We are addicted to control. And we're addicted to the law as a means of control. The problem is, none of us can keep the law.

Titus 3:5-7(NIV) announces: "He saved us, not because of righteous things we had done, but because of his mercy. He saved us through the washing of rebirth and renewal by the Holy Spirit, whom he poured out on us generously through Jesus Christ our Savior, so that, having been justified by his grace, we might become heirs having the hope of eternal life."

Remember how Christianity is spelled. It's not spelled d-o. It is spelled d-o-n-e.

A METAPHOR FROM THE SLAVE MARKET

We were slaves with no hope of release, *but now* we are set free. Romans 3:23-24, "God in His gracious kindness declares us not guilty. He has done this through Christ Jesus, who has *freed us by taking away our sins*." Paul moves from the law court to the slave market. When a slave was redeemed, he was released when a price was paid. We were slaves, but Jesus paid the price to free us from the slavery of sin.

Ephesians 1:7 (NIV) tells us, "In him we have *redemption* through his blood, the forgiveness of sins, in accordance with the riches of God's grace." We must understand that redemption is a gift!

Ninety year-old golf pro Harvey Pennick died a few years ago. His first golf book, *Harvey Pennick's Little Red Book*, sold more than a million copies. In the 1920s, Pennick bought a red spiral notebook and began jotting down observations about golf. He never showed it to anyone except his son until 1991, when Pennick shared it with a writer and asked if he thought it was worth publishing. The man read it and told him "yes." He left word with Pennick's wife the next evening that Simon and Schuster had agreed to an advance of $90,000.

But when the writer saw Pennick later, Pennick seemed troubled. Finally, Harvey came clean. "With all my medical bills," he stated, "there's no way I can advance Simon and Schuster that much money."

The writer quickly explained that Pennick wouldn't be paying Simon and Schuster the money; the publisher would pay him the $90,000. Pennick mistakenly thought the debts was his, but all he had to do was receive.

When it comes to our eternal destiny, sometimes we mistakenly think we have to earn the gift of salvation God offers us. Redemption isn't something we pay for—Christ paid for our redemption at the cross.

We owe God a debt because of our sin. We may wonder why He can't simply forgive our sin debt. If God is really loving and generous, can't He just excuse our repayment? Can He just live and let live?

Author Tim Keller points out that someone always "eats" the cost of sin. Let's say your neighbor crashes his car through your fence. When you discover the shambles, you forgive him: "Don't worry about the fence! All is forgiven." But forgiving your neighbor doesn't do away with the bill or dissolve the damage; forgiveness means you eat the cost.[13]

PRACTICAL STEP: Thank God for the changes He has worked in your life. Then ask Him to continue to work in those areas where you need to keep growing.

Joshua Butler gives another example. Remember the economic crisis in 2008? Banks and financial institutions on Wall Street dropped like flies because fat cat executives, ratings agencies, and the SEC had tolerated subprime loans. Loans were handed out to people who couldn't afford them. When the loans were called in, the housing industry fell apart. Firms like Bear Stearns and AIG went bankrupt, which threw a sledgehammer into the global economy. The stock market went into a nosedive, companies laid off workers, and many people lost their life savings. The nation fell into huge debt.

Someone had to pay the cost. Here's what happened. In the aftermath of the housing crisis, banks were considered "too big to fail." The government forgave the debt, covering the most expensive bailout in human history. Even though the banking industry was the cause of massive damage, the debt was forgiven. But the debt didn't go away. Someone else covered it—in this case, the American people. Someone always eats the cost.[14]

At the cross, God "ate" the cost of our sin. Why can't God just forgive the debt of our sin? Because the debt of sin is devastating. Sin always produces consequences. And more sin. And more consequences. God personally forgave the debt of the world when He covered the cost at the cross.

A METAPHOR FROM WRATH

We were under God's wrath because of sin, *but now* Christ has atoned for our sins. Romans 3:23-24 says, "God in his gracious kindness declares us not guilty. He has done this through Christ Jesus, who freed us by taking away our sins. God sent Jesus to take the punishment for our sins and *to satisfy God's anger against us*. We are made right with God when we believe that Jesus shed his blood, sacrificing his life for us."

Paul starts in the law court. Then he moves to the slave market. Now he moves to the arena of God's wrath against sin. Some theologians find this idea so distasteful that they write it out of scripture. They can't stomach the idea of God expressing wrath against sin.

However, the word *sacrifice* in v. 25 is sometimes translated as "atonement." Atonement means the removal of wrath. Paul has spent the first three chapters of Romans saying that all of humanity stands under God's wrath. His wrath isn't a capricious anger. God doesn't fly off the handle. God doesn't lose His temper. But God is absolutely and adamantly opposed to sin. Sin arouses God's anger in the sense that God hates anything that violates His holiness. He hates anything that stands in the way of what is best for mankind.

But the good news is that when Christ went to the cross, God's wrath was poured out on Christ. Jesus bore the righteous and justified wrath of God against sin so that you and I wouldn't have to bear that wrath! How did this happen? Look at the verse again. "Through the shedding of his blood." The only thing that would avert God's wrath against sin was the blood of Christ. "My hope is built on nothing less than Jesus' blood and righteousness."

"But now" is made possible by the cross. "But now" is not accomplished by the *teachings* of Jesus. Jesus' teachings don't save us. Jesus' instructions are good. They're crucial to understanding who God is and who we are. But His words don't save us. We're not saved by His words—we're saved by His blood! "But now" points to a specific moment in time: Jesus' crucifixion on the cross. The cross is the definitive moment in human history when everything changed, when heaven's court could no longer condemn me. When the slave master could no longer rule me. When the wrath of God could no longer stare me down.

The Chinese language has a fascinating character for the word *righteousness*. It consists of two characters with their own separate meanings. One is the character for the word *lamb*, and the other is the character for the word *me*. In the Chinese language, when you put the word for *lamb* over the character for *me*, you get a brand new word: *righteousness*. That's what righteousness is. It's God sending the lamb and covering me, so that when God looks at me, He sees the righteousness of His Son. That means I can have confidence to live before God every day, because I know that the Lamb has been placed over me.

IS GRACE CARTE BLANCHE?

We might think that our righteousness gives us carte blanche to do whatever we want. We used to be accountable to God, but now we can live any way we want. But this isn't the teaching of scripture. Scripture teaches that there are two different kinds of righteousness: positional righteousness and practical righteousness. Positional righteousness is the right standing we experience before God by grace and through faith. We can do nothing to earn it or to achieve it. Positional righteousness is a gift, plain and simple. We don't get it by achieving, only by believing and receiving. Scripture teaches a second kind of righteousness: practical righteousness, which means living out our position and new identity in Christ. We live in a radically different way, not to earn our salvation, but because we have been saved. Look at these other "but nows" of scripture:

> Romans 6:21-22 (NLT): "And what was the result? You are now ashamed of the things you used to do, things that end in eternal doom. **But now** you are free from the power of sin and have become slaves of God. Now you do those things that lead to holiness and result in eternal life."

> Romans 7:6, **But now** we have been released from the law, for we died to it and are no longer captive to its power. Now we can serve God, not in the old way of obeying the letter of the law, but in the new way of living in the Spirit."

> Ephesians 5:8 (NIV), "For you were once darkness, **but now** you are light in the Lord. Live as children of light."

> Colossians 3:7-8 (NIV), "You used to walk in these ways, in the life you once lived. **But now** you must rid yourselves of all such things as these: anger, rage, malice, slander, and filthy language from your lips."

In other words, grace is not the license to live any way you want. Grace is freedom from the guilt and power of sin.

The cry for forgiveness is not found in performance. It's found by putting our trust in Jesus' performance. Before Christ, we were doomed and damned. We didn't have a chance at eternal life. But now—everything has changed! We have the opportunity to receive forgiveness, to experience what it feels like to have all of our sins forgiven and to live guilt and shame-free lives forever!

PRACTICAL STEP: How did sin affect your past? How does grace affect your future?

Are you ready to fire your inner lawyer—your accuser—who is constantly cross-examining you and pointing out your deficiencies? Why not instead look to Jesus, who offers you a performance-free life that will hold up under all of life's pressures?

CHAPTER TEN

*"In the New Testament grace means God's love in action
towards men who merited the opposite of love.
Grace means God moving heaven and earth to save sinners
who could not lift a finger to save themselves."*
–J. I. Packer

MISSPELLINGS

When I was in first grade, I got tired of standing as I waited at the bus stop, so I sat down. I didn't realize that I'd seated myself on a pile of nasty dog poop.

My folks weren't home, but I knew I had to change. So I raced home, slipped off the soiled pants and put on a clean pair. I hurriedly scribbled a note to my mom so she would know what had happened.

"I WARE BLACK PANS. I SAT IN DOG DEW."

The truth is, I was a pretty good speller. But when you're covered in dog poo and in a panic to get back on the bus, your spelling skills become compromised.

Do you know how to spell Christianity? Most people misspell it. They spell it d-o, when in reality it is spelled d-o-n-e. Salvation is not predicated on what we do—it's predicated on what Christ has done. Consider these passages:

> 2 Timothy 1:9 (NIV): "God saved us and called us to
> a holy life—not because of anything we have done but
> because of his own purpose and grace."

Titus 3:5 (NIV): "He saved us, not because of righteous things we had done, but because of his mercy."

Of all the subjects we need to understand, the place of grace ranks first! At the risk of insulting your intelligence, let me use this chapter to offer an acrostic that spells out g-r-a-c-e. This acrostic is based on Paul's words in the book of Romans.

GIFT

The G in grace stands for *gift*. Romans 3:24 says, "We are justified freely by his grace ..."

Grace is free—it's a gift. We have a hard time with grace because it goes against the grain of our culture. Consider these American phrases:

If it sounds too good to be true, it is.
There's no such thing as a free lunch.
No pain, no gain.
God helps those who help themselves.

Everything about our way of life says that we get what we earn. Grace is counterintuitive. God doesn't give us grace because we deserve it: He just gives it, period.

I have good days and bad days in my spiritual life. Some days I feel pretty good about my walk with God. Other days I mess up big time. So I go from feeling good to feeling bad. I go from congratulating myself to beating myself up, depending on how I've done that day. The problem with that approach is that it all depends on me. If I chin the bar, I feel good. If I don't, I feel bad. But you see, the reality is, I don't ever really chin the bar. I don't ever measure up. Grace says: your relationship with God doesn't depend on your performance. It depends on Jesus' performance.

Comedian Cathy Ladman said: "All religions are the same: religion is basically guilt with different holidays." It's true that many religions spread a message of guilt instead of grace. But grace is what makes Christianity different from every other world religion. Other world religions are based on human achievement. Grace is the one thing the church has to offer that the world can't find anywhere else. A person doesn't have to be a Christian to build homes for the homeless. Or to offer moral instruction. But the one thing we can't find taught anywhere else is grace. Christianity is the only faith that teaches salvation by receiving instead of achieving.

Paul says we are justified freely by His grace. However, we use the word "justified" in different ways. "I felt totally justified in taking the day off." But Paul uses "justified" as a legal term. Paul knows that we are marked by a record: we're guilty of violating God's law. Viewed negatively, justification means God declares us not guilty. Viewed positively, justification means God declares us righteous. God credits us with the righteousness of Jesus.

Paul uses the word "credits" nine times in Romans 4 to describe this exchange. We exchange our sin for Jesus' righteousness. Paul argues that no one can be justified on his own. The Jews tried to justify themselves before God by keeping the law, but they couldn't keep the law. The Gentiles didn't have the law, but they had an innate sense of right and wrong. But they still rejected God and His ways. So everybody stood exposed and guilty before God. Then God stepped in and offered justification. God offered to regard us as justified, just as if we'd never sinned.

Justification deals with all of our sins: past, present and future. When we're justified, our debt is canceled. Our record becomes clean. Some people think of justification as a circle of grace around God. They think they enter the circle when they believe and then they're responsible to keep themselves in the circle. They try to maintain their justification. But when we're justified, we're acquitted and adopted into God's family. No charges against us can stand. Romans 8:33-34 (NIV) says, "Who will bring any charge against those whom God has chosen? It is God who justifies. Who then is the one who condemns? No one."

RECEIVED THROUGH FAITH

The R in grace stands for received. Romans 3:25b says, "to be received by faith ..." The only righteousness we have is by faith. From first to last. From beginning to end. From A to Z.

Picture several different ladders leading to heaven.

Some people think the ladder to heaven is good works.

Some people think the ladder to heaven is Bible knowledge.

Some people think the ladder to heaven is moral goodness.

But there's only one ladder to heaven: faith in the cross of Christ. Do you know why some people refuse to become Christians? They refuse to put their trust in anyone besides themselves! They think, well, I gave to the United Way, so I'm a pretty good person. I love my wife and kids. I don't get drunk or sleep with other people. They put their faith in their goodness.

The problem is that we grossly overestimate our goodness and grossly underestimate the holiness of God. We tend to think that a lie here or a little greed there is no big deal. We think that a little gossip or a little lust are small change to God. But God is so holy and so righteous, that our sins create a huge chasm between Him and us. That's why we can't trust in ourselves.

What are you trusting in? You may be betting the farm that God will let you into heaven based on your goodness. You're risking your eternal soul on the false belief that your good works will get you there. But the only way to heaven is through faith in Jesus Christ.

Faith is believing in certain facts: the death, burial and resurrection of Christ. But faith is much more than mental assent. Faith is trusting that God is able to do what we are powerless to do. It's putting the full weight of our confidence in God. Faith is trusting God and obeying what He tells us to do.

Have you put *your* trust in Christ, and only Christ?

ATONEMENT.

The A in grace stands for atonement. Romans 3:25 says, "God presented Christ as a sacrifice of atonement, through the shedding of his blood ..." This verse explains how God was able to justify sinners. Paul says it was possible because of the "sacrifice of atonement." This phrase comes from a word that was often used to describe turning away the wrath of a god. Many English versions translate the word as "propitiation."

It helps to know the etymology of the word. The Greek word refers to what the New International Version calls the "atonement cover," or the mercy seat. This was the cover of the ark of the covenant where the blood of a sacrificed animal was sprinkled as a means of propitiating God's wrath. For Jews, the atonement cover represented the place where God took care of people's sin problem. Every time we read about an atoning sacrifice, we are reading about an act of grace.

The book of Leviticus drips with grace through atonement, especially in Leviticus 16, where the Day of Atonement is described. The people gathered for the ceremony, which symbolized the removal of their sins. A goat was chosen, known as the scapegoat. All the sins of the people were ceremonially placed on the goat. Then someone was found to lead the goat out of the camp and later out of the city and take the goat away.

The Jews posted watchmen every quarter of a mile outside the city. The watchmen had a runner boy carry news of the progress of the goat into the wilderness back to the people. They would wait until they could no longer see the goat over the crest of the hill for the news to be reported that the goat had taken their sins away.

Sin doesn't simply go away on its own. Someone has to take it away.

No wonder Hebrews 9:14 says, "How much more, then, will the blood of Christ, who through the eternal Spirit offered himself unblemished to God, cleanse our consciences from acts that lead to death, so that we may serve the living God." (NIV) This demonstrates the reality the Day of Atonement pointed to: the blood of Jesus atones for our sins! Nothing covers the cost of our sin except the blood of Jesus. Nothing can absorb the guilt of our sin like the blood of Jesus. The blood of Jesus is the only thing that can break bad!

Let's go back to the word "propitiation" and the idea of turning away the wrath of God. Some people try to sanitize this verse by eliminating reference to the wrath of God; but it's undeniably there. The sacrifice of atonement was necessary because sin arouses the wrath of God. This doesn't mean that God flies off the handle or loses his temper. God's anger is never capricious or arbitrary. He's never malicious, spiteful, or vindictive. His anger is never unpredictable. God's wrath is His steady, unrelenting, uncompromising antagonism against sin. His anger is poles apart from ours.

In the pagan world, human beings tried to avert the wrath of the gods by performing rituals or offering sacrifices. Trying to placate the offended deity. But Paul says there's nothing we can do or say to turn away God's anger. There's no way we can persuade or cajole or bribe God to forgive us. But God took the initiative by his grace to appease his own wrath. God himself presented Jesus as the sacrifice. 1 John 4:10 (NIV), "It is not that we loved God, but that he loved us and sent his Son as a propitiation for our sins." Notice: God's love is the source, not the consequence of the atonement. The atonement didn't procure grace, it flowed from grace. God doesn't love us because Christ died for us—Christ died for us because God loved us.

The sacrifice wasn't an animal or an angel but a divine person: God's Son. God in Christ reconciled the world to Himself. John Stott said: "Thus God took his own loving initiative to appease his own righteous anger by bearing it his own self in his own Son when he took our place and died for us."[15]

A duck hunter was hunting with his friend in the wide-open land of southeastern Georgia. They noticed a cloud of smoke on the horizon. Soon, they could hear the sound of crackling. A wind came up and they realized that a brush fire was headed their way, moving so fast that they couldn't outrun it. One of the men rifled through his pockets and reached for a book of matches. He lit a small fire around the two of them. Soon they were standing in a circle of blackened earth, waiting for the brush fire to come. They covered their mouths with their handkerchiefs and braced themselves. The fire came near-and swept over them, but they were completely unhurt. Fire could not burn the place where fire had already burned.

This is what happens when we're in Christ. If we stand in the shadow of the cross, the death of Christ on the cross acts as our "burned over" place of safety.

When you stand at the cross, you can't be hurt by the fire of God's wrath against sin.

PRACTICAL STEP: Find someone who doesn't know Christ, and explain the gospel to him or her, focusing especially on God's grace.

CHRIST

The C in grace stands for Christ. Romans 3:25b-26 (NIV), "He did this to demonstrate his righteousness, because in his forbearance he had left the sins committed beforehand unpunished—he did it to demonstrate his righteousness at the present time, so as to be just and the one who justifies those who have faith in Jesus."

God can't condone sin. He doesn't bend the rules or neglect the evidence. He doesn't lower His standards. God justifies us on the basis of perfect obedience and a perfect sacrifice. But the obedience and the sacrifice are not ours, they are Christ's. The Bible says that God Himself paid that penalty in the person of His own Son.

2 Corinthians 5: 21 (The Message) says, "God put the wrong on him who never did anything wrong, so we could be put right with God." God placed our sins on Jesus, so we could be reconciled to God.

But why was the sacrifice of atonement necessary? Because God had to demonstrate His justice. In the Old Testament period, God didn't punish sins with the severity that sin deserved. People who sinned should have suffered spiritual death, because no sacrifice existed to atone for their sins. But in his mercy God "passed over" their sins. His holy character means that He can't overlook sin, that He has to punish sin. So when Christ came, He satisfied God's justice. Christ paid for the sins of all people—both before His lifetime and after His lifetime.

People often ask, *How were people in the Old Testament saved—people who lived before Christ?* They were saved the same way you and I are saved: by faith. They trusted that God would do what He said He would do: provide a sufficient sacrifice for their sins.

When people in the Old Testament put their faith in God, they received salvation that comes through faith. Was their salvation paid for at that time? No, but their faith looked forward to the time when Christ would make the payment. He would offer himself and pay for sin. So those who put their faith in God and trusted Him were saved, even though the payment would be made later.

Imagine a great and generous king. He hears that his subjects have revolted. He sends messengers to check it out. The rebels kill them. So he sends his own dear son, the prince. They murder him viciously: they hang his body on the city wall. What would you expect the king to do now? Send his armies and take revenge, right? He has the right and the power to avenge himself.

But what if the king turned around and offered the criminals a full pardon? What if he said, "I will accept my son—whom you murdered—as the payment for all your rebellion. You can go free. All I require is that you admit your wrongs and trust in my son's purchase of your forgiveness." But the king isn't finished. He says, "I invite you to come live in my palace, eat at my table, and enjoy all the benefits of the kingdom. I'll adopt you as my children and make you my heirs. Everything that's mine is now yours."

God doesn't condone our sin, or compromise His standard. He doesn't ignore our rebellion or relax His demands. Instead of dismissing our sin, He assumes our sin. He sentences Himself. God does what we can't do so we can be what we dare not dream: perfect in His eyes. The cross is where love and justice meet. There is no grace without the cross!

EQUALITY BEFORE GOD

The E in grace stands for equality before God. Romans 3:27 tells us, "Where, then, is boasting? It is excluded. Because of what law? The law that requires works? No, because of the law that requires faith. For we maintain that a person is justified by faith apart from the works of the law." This is one of the great teachings of Romans. The ground is level at the foot of the cross.

In Romans Paul uses a question and answer format. He wants everyone to understand that since God saves people by grace, No one can take credit for salvation. The Jews had a tendency to boast in the works of the law. But Paul says that works do not matter. We cannot be saved by works; we are saved by grace. Nothing eliminates pride like grace. This is why Paul is so adamant about teaching grace to the Roman church! No one has bragging rights! It's futile for anyone to brag about their works when works cannot achieve a righteous standing before God! Grace means equality before God.

A few years ago, I preached about stewardship one Sunday morning. I explained that "Holly and I would like to be able to buy a home computer, but we feel like we can't do that without compromising our plan for giving and saving." I didn't think much about the remark at the time. That night, I preached again. After the evening church service, a little girl greeted me as I was walking down the aisle. She handed me a note, which I tucked into my pocket.

Once everyone was gone, I went to my car, slipped behind the wheel, and opened the note. It was written by the little girl's parents.

"We had been planning to expand our home computer system, but when we heard your message, we decided to fund a computer for you instead."

With the note was a check for $2000! I was blown away.

Two days later, I visited the local computer store. I ordered a computer and a printer and paid by way of the couple's generous gift. When I got home, my wife Holly pointed to two boxes sitting in the entryway of our house. I said, "What are those?" We opened the boxes. As it turned out, a former member of our church, who had since moved to Baltimore, had listened to the same Sunday morning stewardship message two days prior, via the Internet. After hearing the message, the former member had boxed up his nearly-new computer and printer and shipped them to our home in Dallas. I hustled to get off the phone and cancel the computer ordered at the store earlier that morning.

I was enormously grateful! Laughing to myself, I thought, *The next time I preach on stewardship, I'm going to say, "Holly and I would really like a new car, but we feel like we can't buy one without compromising our plan for giving and saving!"*

Seriously, we didn't deserve the generous gift of the computer and printer. We couldn't have earned or paid for either. They came to us strictly because of the donor's generosity.

So it is with grace. God did for us what we could never accomplish on our own.

Complete the following, according to this chapter:

G_____

R_____

A_____

C_____

E_____

Part Three

GRACE: WHAT DIFFERENCE DOES IT MAKE?

CHAPTER ELEVEN

"All human nature vigorously resists grace
because grace changes us and the change is painful."
—Flannery O'Connor

GRACISM

Benjamin Watson was a tight end for the New Orleans Saints who witnessed the racial unrest and conflict in Ferguson, Missouri. A grand jury chose not to indict a white police officer who was investigated for shooting a black man during a police-citizen altercation. Anger flooded through Ferguson as black people looted the city, and white people questioned why the police officer's story was questioned.

Watson also observed the backlash in the wake of the grand jury decision. His heart hurt over the chaos and outrage. The day following the decision he wrote a Facebook post that went viral in a few hours.

"I'M ENCOURAGED, because ultimately the problem is not a SKIN problem; it is a SIN problem. SIN is the reason we rebel against authority. SIN is the reason we abuse our authority. SIN is the reason we are racist, prejudiced, and lie to cover for our own. SIN is the reason we riot, loot, and burn. BUT I'M ENCOURAGED because God has provided a solution for sin through His son Jesus and with it, a transformed heart and mind."[1]

Watson was accurate in his assessment. The real problem regarding racial tension is not a skin problem, but a sin problem. Whenever people choose to hate each other and retaliate against each other, the root problem is sin. This is a not only a serious issue for communities where race relations are obviously strained. Racial bias can exist in any community and be a problem in any heart. Prejudice is not an issue that is limited to the national news, but is an issue that breaks the heart of God. God is passionate about His children honoring one another. What matters to God must matter to us, and racial issues matter to God.

The more I've looked at grace, the more I've realized a powerful connection exists between grace and race. I'm convinced if we really understand grace, it will make a huge difference in the way we deal with matters of race.

I hate racism and prejudice, but when I look at my response to racism in light of grace, I clearly see that God is calling me to do more. I'm challenged. When we embrace grace, we change how we respond to race.

To better understand grace and race, let's look at three episodes in the life of the Apostle Peter.

GOD'S GRACE NEVER SHOWS PARTIALITY

God's grace spells the end to discrimination and prejudice. God never limits His grace to people of a certain color. Peter found this out in Acts 10. This is a text where religious prejudice and racial prejudice are viewed as one. Tension exists between Jews and Gentiles. Peter is a Jew and Cornelius is a Gentile. The two men not only had different religious views, they also had different racial backgrounds. The Jews historically viewed Gentiles as outsiders and aliens to God's kingdom.

But God sends Peter on a mission to the Gentiles. He wants Peter and Cornelius and all the world to know that God shows no partiality. So God tells Peter to go to the house of Cornelius. Peter considered Cornelius "off-limits" for two reasons: first, Cornelius was the wrong race. He was a Gentile, a non-Jew. Second, since he was a non-Jew, he was an outsider. He wasn't part of God's chosen people. Everybody knew that Jews and non-Jews lived on opposite sides of town.

God gives Peter a strange vision. A sheet is let down from heaven containing all kinds of animals that the Jews considered unclean: pigs, snakes, storks, bats, beetles, and bears. The voice in the vision says, "Get up, Peter, kill and eat." Peter responds, "Wait a minute, God, I've never eaten anything impure or unclean." The voice answers, "Don't call anything impure that God has made clean." This was God's way of saying, "Peter, don't consider the Gentiles unclean. I'm inviting the Gentiles into my kingdom too, and I want you to deliver the invitation!"

So Peter answers the call. Acts 10:34 tells us, "I now realize how true it is that God does not show favoritism but accepts men from every nation who fear him and do what is right." (NIV) Did you hear that? God doesn't play favorites. God won't tolerate an attitude of racism. He won't tolerate whites hating blacks and blacks hating whites. He won't tolerate whites hating people of Middle Eastern descent and people of Middle Eastern descent hating whites. The reason God doesn't show partiality is because of grace! Peter was bigoted because he thought he was the insider and Cornelius was the outsider, but God showed him differently!

Peter thought he was better because he honored the Jewish rules of the law—things like circumcision and the Sabbath and certain dietary laws. But God was in the process of teaching Peter an important lesson. First, those laws were never designed to be the way to salvation. And second, those laws were superseded by the promise that God would give the gift of salvation to anyone who believed, Jew or Gentile. So God comes and says, "Peter, acceptance isn't based on keeping the rules. It's based on faith. You need to know that I'm accepting Cornelius because of his faith."

God's acceptance isn't based on anything external. Jesus was not Caucasian! God loves every person, no matter what their color. God is not only colorblind, He is colorful. Grace isn't based on color or economic status or education or the neighborhood you live in. God's grace never discriminates! God's grace never shows partiality.

> PRACTICAL STEP: Read Martin Luther King's *Letter from Birmingham Jail.*

PREJUDICE IS THE DEADLY ENEMY OF GRACE

In Acts 10, Peter comes to understand that the gospel is for everyone. Then he starts backpedaling. Fast forward to Galatians 2. The scene switches to Antioch, where Peter is eating with Gentiles. He enjoys big meals with ham and pork chops and bacon. He knows it's ok to eat those things, and he knows God wants him to have lunch with Gentiles.

But then, one day, the religious police come to town. The rule-keeping racists show up. They're sniffing around to see if anybody has ham on his breath. They've put a ban on bacon and a pox on pork. Even though Peter has said the right thing in Acts 15, now he fails to practice what he'd preached. He backs down because of the pressure of some of his Jewish friends. Peter says to his Gentile buddies, "Sorry, I can't have lunch with you today." He pulls back from his Gentile friends because he's afraid of the Jewish discriminators. Peter might have gotten away with it if it hadn't been for Paul. Paul came and saw what was going on.

And Paul didn't beat around the bush. He got right in Peter's face. He said, Peter, you're a hypocrite. You eat with the Gentiles when the rule-keepers and racists aren't around. But when the legalists come around, you chicken out. You go back to partiality. You go back to discrimination.

Listen to how upset Paul was about this. Galatians 2:11-14 says (The Message), "Later, when Peter came to Antioch, I had a face-to-face confrontation with him because he was clearly out of line. Here's the situation. Earlier, before certain persons had come from James, Peter regularly ate with the non-Jews. But when that conservative group came from Jerusalem, he cautiously pulled back and put as much distance as he could manage between himself and his non-Jewish friends. That's how fearful he was of the conservative Jewish clique that's been pushing the old system of circumcision.

"Unfortunately, the rest of the Jews in the Antioch church joined in that hypocrisy so that even Barnabas was swept along in the charade. But when I saw that they were not maintaining a steady, straight course according to the Message, I spoke up to Peter in front of them all: "If you, a Jew, live like a non-Jew when you're not being observed by the watchdogs from Jerusalem, what right do you have to require non-Jews to conform to Jewish customs just to make a favorable impression on your old Jerusalem cronies?"

Paul knew Peter was compromising the very truth of the gospel. Paul knew that partiality is the deadly enemy of grace. So Paul let Peter have it. He said, "Peter, you know we're saved by grace. So how can you force rule-keeping on the Gentiles? And how can you draw back from Gentile believers? Partiality shuts the door: grace opens the door. Partiality excludes: grace includes." Peter forgot the lesson God taught him in Acts 10. So Paul got in his face about grace and race! He didn't call for a workshop on race relations. He didn't have a seminar on unity. He opposed Peter to his face!

Tony Evans preaches for Oak Cliff Bible Fellowship in Dallas. A lot of white people started coming to their church. One of their black members was getting unhappy. He said, "Pastor, I'm upset. We've got too many whites coming to our church. And you know how they are. After a while they're going to try and take over." Tony said, "Well, then you better do a lot of black evangelism then and keep blacks coming in here." The man said, "Well, I don't like it and I'm leaving." Tony said, "Bye." Tony didn't need a seminar or a sensitivity session. He just needed the word of God and the Word of God had already told him what to say.

We may know racism is sinful and wrong. But then somebody comes around with a racist attitude, and we start to waffle. We let their prejudice influence what we think and what we do. Paul says, if you do that, you compromise the very truth of the gospel! Don't let legalism destroy the gospel. Don't let racism destroy the gospel, because partiality is a poison that wrecks the truth of the gospel.

WHEN WE REALLY "GET" GRACE

Now fast forward to Acts 15. Lots of Gentiles are coming into the church, right and left. Non-Jews are being saved by God's grace. But there were some people who were really ticked off about the message of grace. They were believers who said, "You know, grace is fine, but if you really want to be a Christian, you have to keep the law of Moses. It isn't enough to believe in Christ. You have to keep the law. You're not a Christian if you're not circumcised, if you don't keep the law of Moses, and if you don't become a Jew!"

In Acts 15, the apostles and elders came to Jerusalem to talk about this issue. Peter stood up and said words that every Christian needs to hear: "Brothers, you know that some time ago God made a choice among you that the Gentiles might hear from my lips the message of the gospel and believe. God, who knows the heart, showed that he accepted them by giving the Holy Spirit to them, just as he did to us. *He made no distinction between us and them*, for he purified their hearts by faith. Now then, why do you try to test God by putting on the necks of the disciples a yoke that neither we nor our fathers have been able to bear?

No! We believe *it is through the grace of our Lord Jesus that we are saved,* just as they are." Acts 15:6-11 (NIV)

Peter makes it clear: not only does grace eliminate the barrier that stood between us and God but grace eliminates barriers between us and people of other races. Anyone who is saved is saved by the grace of God, no matter what their color. We must be careful that we do not build walls where God builds bridges. The ground is level at the foot of the cross.

Are you letting race become a barrier? Do you believe that people of every race and color are equal before God? Do you live out that truth? Are you doing everything you can to eliminate racism in your life, the lives of your kids, and the lives of people around you?

Dr. Patricia Raybon is a black woman who wrote a book called *My First White Friend.*[17] She talks about how she hated white people until God convicted her. God showed her how wrong her attitude was. She repented. She realized she was saved by grace. And since she was saved by grace, she had to extend grace to everyone—including white people. When we really "get" grace, we're willing to give it to everyone. We don't hold back because of someone's color or nationality. We give grace freely, regardless of race or background.

I believe God calls us to make three statements to those of a different race.

"I AM LISTENING"

Discrimination may not appear as blatant as it was a few years ago, but bigotry is alive and well. Both white people and African-Americans believe that racism is a continuing issue. A majority of Americans say racism remains a major problem in American society and politics, according to an NBC News poll. Overall, 64 percent said racism remains a major problem in our society. Thirty percent agreed that racism exists today, but it isn't a major problem.[18]

We can't begin to understand and respect each other until and unless we first begin to listen to each other.

Wayburn Dean is a black Christian vocalist. I talked to Wayburn about race relations. He said, "You know, most white Christians really have no idea what it's like to be black in America. They have no idea how much discrimination is still out there." He didn't ask me to be a crusader, but he did urge me to be a listener and to be proactive in trying to understand what it's like to experience discrimination.

I read about a 16 year-old black teenager who didn't want to get his driver's license because he'd watched his father be stopped by police over and over for no cause. The teen figured that if it happened to his dad, it would certainly happen to him.

I learned of a student attending a Christian university. She was serving as a dorm assistant on campus. When all the kids were moving into the dorm, a white girl and a black girl were assigned to be roommates. When the father of the white girl found out, he threw a fit. He was furious that his daughter would be sharing a room with a black student. As it turned out, the white girl had no problem with have a black roommate at all. Soon the girls enjoyed a great relationship. But the father's attitude demonstrated that racism is alive and kicking.

A few years ago I talked with an African American man in our church. He told me that someone had come at night and cut the wires to his Christmas lights. So he repaired the lights and put them up again. Someone came along and cut the wires again. My friend lives in a predominantly white neighborhood. "I asked him, do you think it was racially motivated?" He said, "I don't know. But my mother taught me to be humble and to ask God to keep me from a spirit of resentment."

We may think racism isn't a problem because we no longer see separate restrooms and water fountains. But racism doesn't have to be overt or brutal to be oppressive. Discrimination is often subtle and covert. But God is passionate about this issue. Paul said, "There is neither Jew nor Greek, slave nor free, male nor female." (Galatians 3:28) (NIV) He would add, there is neither black nor white, nor Asian nor Hispanic, nor rich nor poor.

We need to intentionally listen to people of other races and those who are different from us. We need to find out what it's like to live in their skin. We must do this without making it an item on an agenda. Forced love is not love at all. We must work to forge genuine relationships out of sincere desire to know our brothers.

We need to empathize with people who have lived lives different from our own. What is it like to grow up in a neighborhood where textbooks are outdated and shared among students? What is it like to be doubted, disbelieved, dismissed, and disrespected because of the color of your skin? We need to be willing to say, "I am listening."

One day theologian Miroslav Volf was visiting a friend who pastors a church in Sandtown, a desperately poor and dangerous neighborhood in Baltimore. Volf's friend talked about the real hope for Sandtown—justification by faith. Volf thought, most people never apply that biblical doctrine to problems like poverty and hopelessness. But then Volf reflected: "Imagine that you have no job, no money, you live cut off from the rest of society in a world ruled by poverty and violence, your skin is the "wrong" color—and you have no hope that any of this will change. Around you is a society governed by the iron law of achievement. You are a failure, and you know that you will continue to be a failure because there is no way to achieve tomorrow what you have not managed to achieve today. Your dignity is shattered and your soul is enveloped in the darkness of despair.

"But the gospel tells you that you are not defined by outside forces. It tells you that you count; even more that you are loved unconditionally and infinitely, irrespective of anything you have achieved or failed to achieve. Imagine now this gospel not simply proclaimed but embodied in a community. Justified by sheer grace, it seeks to "justify" by grace those declared "unjust" by a society's implacable law of achievement ... This is justification by grace, proclaimed and practiced. A dead doctrine? Hardly!"[19]

"I AM SORRY"

You may be saying, "I haven't done anything to hurt people of other races. Why should I have to apologize for something I didn't do?" We don't have to take personal responsibility for all the racial wrongs in America, but we should feel ashamed of the history of racism in this country. I am ashamed that African Americans were kidnapped, shackled in the holds of slave ships, and forced to work for almost nothing. I am ashamed that in many cities in America, minorities are still treated shabbily.

A few years ago, Abilene Christian University did the right thing. There was a time in the history of ACU when black students were shunned. When black preachers weren't invited to speak on campus. When the university, by its silence, endorsed racism. But years ago, the administration at ACU issued a public statement. They said in essence, "We're sorry for the discrimination we've contributed to. We're sorry for the horrible way we sometimes treated people of other races." The university not only said, "We're sorry." It took specific steps to make sure acts of discrimination wouldn't happen again!

There are times when it's appropriate to say, "I am sorry—I am sorry for the discrimination you have suffered at the hands of others simply because of your race."

"I WILL GET INVOLVED"

Giving grace to others means we must go beyond words. Jesus said, here's the greatest command: Love God with all of your heart, soul, mind, and strength. And the second is like it: love your neighbor as yourself. Do you hear what Jesus is saying? We only love God to the extent we love other people!

Dorothy Day once said, "I really only love God as much as I love the person I love the least." When we think of the person or the people we love the least, that's how much we love God! If we hold back, we don't love God as much as we say we do! How can we claim to be Christians if we pick and choose who we're going to love!

What does this mean at a practical level? It means inviting people of other races into our home. Most of us automatically invite people we know best to come over for burgers. But I want to challenge all of us: instead of inviting people who look like us talk like us over for a backyard barbecue, invite a family of another race or culture. Reach across the barriers that keep us apart.

In the middle of the eighteenth century, British Christians became increasingly concerned about the slave trade. They tried to overcome the slave trade interests in Parliament, but they needed political leadership. William Wilberforce was elected to Parliament in 1780. He was converted in 1785 and began the battle against slavery. He met fierce resistance from slave traders, who had powerful allies in Parliament. But with the help of Christians throughout England, Wilberforce eventually succeeded. And in 1807 Parliament voted to abolish the slave trade. We need people like William Wilberforce—Christians who are willing to carry out an aggressive and sustained fight against racism.

Jackie Robinson was the first black to play major league baseball. While breaking baseball's "color barrier," he faced jeering crowds in every stadium. While playing one day in his home stadium in Brooklyn, he committed an error. His own fans began to ridicule him. He stood at second base, humiliated, while the fans jeered. Then shortstop "Pee Wee" Reese came over and stood next to him. He put his arm around Jackie Robinson and faced the crowd. The fans grew quiet. Robinson later said that arm around his shoulder saved his career.

As I've thought about prejudice, God has shown me that I have a long way to go. I don't actively discriminate against people of other colors and nationalities. But the truth is, I haven't done much to build bridges to them, either. Racial tension is not a skin problem; it's a sin problem! The only answer to the sin problem of race is the gospel of grace!

What matters to God has to matter to us. Someday we're going to stand before God, and He's going to ask us, what did you do with my grace? I gave it to you freely; how well did you do in giving it away? I can think of few things as important to God as establishing justice and building bridges to people of other races. Revelation 7 says that in heaven, people from every nation, tribe, people, and language will stand before the throne of God in worship and praise. Someday we'll join in worship with people of every color, and we'll give an account to Jesus who died to save the world. He will ask, "Did you extend my grace to people of every race?"

PRACTICAL STEP: If you are aware of systemic racism in your company, your school, or your neighborhood, ask God to reveal ways you can counter such practices. Then, go to work to oppose and change any structural inequities that exist.

CHAPTER TWELVE

"I do not at all understand the mystery of grace -
only that it meets us where we are
but does not leave us where it found us."
—**Anne Lamott**

JUSTICE

We typically think of grace as a *current* reality that results in forgiveness. This is true, but grace also includes a future dimension. God's grace points to a future time when all of the forces that have ever wounded us will meet justice. Ultimately, God's grace will turn the tables on evil and vindicate believers in Christ.

Colossians 2:13-15 (NLT) says, "You were dead because of your sins and because your sinful nature was not yet cut away. Then God made you alive with Christ, for he forgave all our sins. He canceled the record of the charges against us and took it away by nailing it to the cross. In this way, he disarmed the spiritual rulers and authorities. He shamed them publicly by his victory over them on the cross."

THE CRY FOR JUSTICE

Our world is screaming for justice. We witness photos of a deadly gas attack on civilians in Syria. Millions of Syrian refugees are driven from their homes and flee across Europe. Countless boys and girls are kidnapped and abducted every year and sold into sexual slavery. Our world cries out for justice.

A common street chant of our times is "no justice, no peace." For some of us, the cry for justice is extremely personal. We were raped, and the rapist was never prosecuted. We were slandered and our name sullied, and the slander was never confronted. We were cheated: out of money, out of an opportunity, out of a relationship. For as long as humanity has populated the earth, wrong has been left unrighted. God is passionate about justice. God is outraged by injustice! God doesn't lose His temper. He is adamantly opposed to injustice and absolutely committed to righting wrongs.

But where is God's wrath against injustice most graphically displayed? Fleming Rutledge has pointed out that God's wrath against injustice is most shockingly demonstrated at the cross.[20] Who would have imagined that God would vent His opposition to injustice at the cross? Who would have thought that God would intervene by offering Himself—that God would unleash His wrath against wrong on Himself at the cross?

We often think of the cross as an answer to man's cry for forgiveness. Yes, the cross offers that answer, but it goes beyond forgiveness. As someone has said, forgiveness is not enough. Something is wrong with our world, and it cries out to be made right.

In Colossians 2, Paul addresses both the world's cry for forgiveness *and* their cry for justice. He begins with the cry for forgiveness in verse 14: "He canceled the record of the charges against us and took it away by nailing it to the cross." (NLT) An incriminating list of unpaid debts indicted us. The penalty for not paying those debts was death.

But God did more than just take our IOU and throw it away. He made full payment on our behalf at the cross. When a man was crucified in biblical times, charges against him were posted above his head. When Jesus went to the cross, He paid that sin debt for us! He was condemned so we wouldn't have to be.

Ironically, when we typically talk about injustice, we think about injustices others have committed *against us.* However, every injustice we ever committed was committed *against Jesus.* Yet He paid the price of our sin committed in rebellion against Him. He not only paid a price we could not pay because of His divine nature, but that we refused to pay because of our sinful nature.

But Jesus did so much more than that! Look at verse 15 (NLT): "In this way, he disarmed the spiritual rulers and authorities. He shamed them publicly by his victory over them on the cross." Something amazing was going on behind the scenes. The cross was a frontal assault on injustice. Jesus attacked spiritual rulers and authorities! But who does this refer to?

Galatians 4:3 describes these forces at work to enslave and control our world through demonic forces who destroy justice. Ephesians 6 describes them as the powers of this dark world. These Satanic rulers and authorities are radically opposed to the purposes of God. They wreak havoc and destruction wherever they go. They are dictators and drug lords. Corrupt corporations. Gangs. Employers who exploit their workers. Bullies at school. Agents of evil.

But Paul says that through the cross, Christ did three things to subdue the agents of injustice.

CHRIST DISARMED THE RULERS AND AUTHORITIES

Christ disarmed rulers and authorities. Literally, He denuded them and stripped them of their power and importance. The irony is that Jesus did to the rulers what they had done to him. The Roman soldiers dragged him through the streets and then stripped him naked and nailed Him to the cross. It looked like they had stripped Him, but in reality Jesus was exposing them!

CHRIST SHAMED THE RULERS AND AUTHORITIES

Christ publicly shamed the rulers and authorities. He made a public spectacle of them by parading them through the streets. Jesus leveraged the atrocity of the cross against the rulers of this world. His death and resurrection left the rulers helpless.

CHRIST TRIUMPHED OVER THE RULERS AND AUTHORITIES

Christ triumphed over them. He marched them through the streets in a triumphal procession. Ephesians 4 says that Christ led captives in His train. There is graphic irony here. When Rome defeated an enemy, they marched their victims through the streets to show that they were defeated. Christ parades the rulers through the streets to demonstrate His victory! The conquerors have been conquered!

Matt Woodley points to an analogy. Imagine a soldier has fallen behind enemy lines and been taken captive. His captors surround him, spit on him, and mock him. But the mocking isn't enough; they beat him. At first they take turns, but as their rage and hatred grows, they go at him all at the same time, punching and kicking and cursing him uncontrollably. The fallen soldier won't go down, so they continue to torture him. As they continue to beat him, they cannot contain themselves. They're flooded with sadism and cruelty. The sludge of evil in their hearts pours out, and they are exposed for what they are. Finally, as the beating continues, they kill the prisoner. He falls, dead at last. The captors are relived and spent. They slump to the ground, exhausted.

Unexpectedly, a few days later, the dead soldier stands up again. He's alive! The captors can't believe it. They spewed all of their evil at him, but he's back. The process of killing their captive had made the men falsely feel in charge. When the soldier fell to the ground, they believed they had finished him off for good. But the soldier had actually routed them! He had declawed sin and death. Similarly but on a far greater scale, Jesus stripped the powers of darkness and death through His crucifixion. He won the victory over sin and evil.[21]

The first announcement that rulers and authorities had been disarmed was the resurrection. The resurrection confirmed Jesus' victory over the agents of injustice. The resurrection declared that Jesus had sent the forces of injustice to defeat. The resurrection was the conquest confirmed and announced. The resurrection was the victory endorsed and proclaimed. The rulers and authorities had been overcome.

Yes, unjust things happen in the world that we can't explain and don't understand. Tragedies and outrages happen everywhere. Life on earth is a tangle of broken stories that all lead to a divine ending. The day is coming when justice will be served.

Acts 17:31 (NIV), "For he has set a day when he will judge the world with *justice* by the man he has appointed. He has given proof of this to everyone by raising him from the dead." The cross and resurrection prove that no matter how bad things get, we can trust God. But we have to be honest. We can affirm the cross and the resurrection, but the world is still throbbing with pain. Children are still neglected. Spouses suffer abuse. The poor are overlooked. And people of faith are often mistreated. We must remember that we live between the already and the not yet. Although rulers and authorities have been defeated, the final outcome is something we still await.

ALREADY BUT NOT YET

Satan has been defeated, but he hasn't conceded. He's been overthrown, but not eliminated. This is the tension we live in. Rulers and authorities have been disarmed, but they're still trying to overcome those who put their trust in God. The paradox is that even though Christ has won the victory, mopping-up operations must still be done. The devil has been dethroned, but he hasn't changed his strategy. He's still persecuting Christians around the world. He's working to keep injustice alive. While we need to recognize Satan's power, we don't need to fear him. We need to put on the full armor of God, so we can stand against him. Eph. 6:10 tells us, "For our battle is not against flesh and blood, but against the rulers, against the authorities, against the powers of this dark world and against the spiritual forces of evil in the heavenly realms." Christ disarmed the rulers and authorities of this world!

WHEN HE COMES AGAIN!

Jesus' victory over the forces of injustice will be consummated when He comes again! The Bible is clear that when Jesus returns, His reign will be complete. Christ already reigns, but the day is coming when death itself will be defeated once and for all. The day is coming when every knee will bow and every tongue confess that Jesus is Lord, Phil. 2:10. (NIV) The day is coming when the devil will be thrown into the lake of fire, Rev. 20:10. (NIV) Look at 1 Corinthians 15:24-25 (NIV): "Then the end will come, when he hands over the kingdom to God the Father after he has destroyed all dominion, authority and power. For he must reign until he has put all his enemies under his feet."

John Lennox tells about touring Eastern Europe and meeting a Jewish woman from South Africa. The woman told Lennox that she was researching how her relatives had perished in the Holocaust. At one point on their guided tour, there were pictures of Nazi atrocities. At that point of their tour, the Jewish woman turned to Lennox and said, "And what does your religion make of this?" Lennox said, "I have no easy answers; but I do have what, for me at least, is a doorway into an answer." "What is it?" she said. I said, "You know that I am a Christian. That means that I believe that Yeshua is the messiah. I also believe that he was God incarnate, come into our world as savior, which is what his name 'Yeshua' means. Now I know that this is even more difficult for you to accept. Nevertheless, just think about this question—if Yeshua was really God, as I believe he was, what was God doing on a cross?

"Could it be that God begins just here to meet our heartbreaks, by demonstrating that he did not remain distant from our human suffering, but became part of it himself? For me, this is the beginning of hope; and it is a living hope that cannot be smashed by the enemy of death. The story does not end in the darkness of the cross. Yeshua conquered death. He rose from the dead; and one day, as the final judge, he will assess everything in absolute fairness, righteousness, and mercy."

"There was silence. She was still standing, arms outstretched, forming a motionless cross in the doorway. After a moment, with tears in her eyes, very quietly but audibly, she said: 'Why has no one ever told me that about my messiah before?'"[22]

We may think of Jesus' return as a moment of great joy and victory. And it will be. But for agents of injustice, it will be a horrible day. Revelation 16 describes how God will pour out seven bowls of wrath on those who have persecuted Christians. Justice is coming for those who have suffered for the faith! Wrongs will be righted!

Christopher Wright tells about a friend from India who was led to Christ by reading the Old Testament. His friend had grown up among the despised Dalit (outcast) community in his village. His family had suffered at the hands of the high-caste Hindus in the village—all kinds of violence and injustice. He wanted to get revenge against his oppressors. One day he started reading the Bible. He opened it at random and started reading the story of Naboth and Ahab in 1 Kings 21. This is the story of the unjust King Ahab who uses his power to steal the land from Naboth, an ordinary farmer. As the man read, he thought, *This was my story*. His family had experienced theft of land, false accusations, and even murder.

But then he read on and was amazed to read about another man called Elijah. Elijah denounced King Ahab, and said that he would be judged and punished by this God. And the man found this astounding! "My friend had millions of gods within Hinduism to choose from. But he had never heard of such a god as he was reading about in this Bible. Here was a god who took the side of the suffering ones and condemned the government and the powerful for their wicked deeds. "I never knew such a god existed" were his exact words to me, which I have never forgotten. As this man continued to read the Bible, he learned about Jesus, his life and death and resurrection. He also learned about the need to forgive. But his road to conversion started by meeting the God who is just and who takes the side of the oppressed.[23]

JOINING IN THE MISSION OF THE CHURCH

Part of the mission of the church is to join Christ in the fight against injustice. You can join the fight for justice by participating in justice-serving ministries by serving the homeless. By visiting and teaching those in prison. By providing meals for underprivileged children. By joining the fight against sexual slavery. By looking for opportunities to serve the poor and marginalized.

You can be an agent of grace by partnering with International Justice Mission and other ministries that battle slavery all over the world. Maybe the worst cases of injustice in our world today are forced labor slavery and sexual slavery. Forced labor slavery uses deception, threats, or violence to coerce someone to work for little to no pay. Even though slavery has been outlawed in nearly every country, millions of men, women and children are working as slaves. There are an estimated 46 million people held in slavery today. Children represent an estimated 26% of all forced labor victims. Forced labor slavery is a violent crime. Physical and sexual assault are rampant. Forced labor slaves have been beaten, gang raped, locked in tiny rooms, starved and even killed. Victims who try and escape often report being tracked down, beaten and returned to the facility.

You can join the fight for justice by opposing racism whenever you see it! David Anderson challenges us to move from racism to gracism.[24] Racism is speaking, acting or thinking negatively about someone else solely based on that person's color, class or culture. We need to replace racism with gracism! A gracist reaches across ethnic lines to extend extra grace to those who are different or marginalized. A gracist builds bridges of inclusion. Are you a gracist? "If you really keep the royal law found in Scripture, 'Love your neighbor as yourself,' you are doing right. But if you show favoritism, you sin and are convicted by the law as lawbreakers." (James 2:8-9, NIV)

It's easy to look at a world filled with violence, cruelty, and hatred and conclude that evil has won the day. But Colossians 2 turns all of these things upside down. Colossians 2 reminds us that Jesus is the real victor. Jesus stripped rulers and authorities of their power. He paraded them through the streets. He triumphed over them! What appeared to be defeat was actually victory. What appeared to be loss was actually gain.

Right now you might be experiencing evil. You might be suffering from injustice. Maybe you've been abused, or you are being abused. Maybe you're being exploited. Maybe someone you know and love is being taken advantage of. Maybe as you look at what's going on in the world, your heart is ripped to pieces. You hear the cries of refugees pleas for justice. Maybe you're guilty of committing injustice. You've mistreated people you should have loved. You overlooked injustice going on right under your nose. You failed to speak up when you should have spoken up.

GUILTY OF INJUSTICE?
CONFESS IT TO GOD

If we're guilty of injustice, we need to confess it to God and claim His forgiveness. We need to realize that He paid the debt we can't pay. We need to come to Him for salvation! If we're wounded by injustice, we need to take heart. We need to realize the day is coming when all wrongs will be made right. All injustice will be eliminated, and Christ will put rulers and authorities down to defeat once and for all!

Maybe it appears that injustice has the upper hand, and you're discouraged. It feels like there's no justice for malicious people, unjust rulers, and sin-seeking authorities. Look to the cross. And affirm the fact that Jesus conquered sin and injustice. What we see is temporary. When Christ comes again, the great rider on the white horse will trample rulers and authorities and all who practice injustice into the ground. He will shut them down and shut them up, never to be heard from again!

Jesus experienced the most potent concentration of pure evil that this world has ever produced; its diabolical force took his life; but ultimately, Jesus rose again to new life. The grave couldn't hold Him. No evil power could hold Him. The jaws of hell couldn't hold him, and although these forces can intimidate and frighten us, they cannot and never will be able to destroy us if we are God's redeemed.

Grace doesn't end with this life. Grace points to a future when all wrongs will be reversed and the demands of justice will be satisfied!

PRACTICAL STEP: Contact World Vision or Christian Relief Fund or another organization that serves the needs of orphans. Support an orphan each month with your finances and prayers. You can also be an agent of grace by partnering with International Justice Mission and other ministries that battle slavery all over the world.

CHAPTER THIRTEEN

*"Grace is the voice that calls us to change
and then gives us the power to pull it off."*
−Max Lucado

MORPHING

Solomon Northup's *12 Years a Slave* tells the author's life story as a free black man from the North. Northrup was kidnapped and sold into slavery in the pre-Civil War South. He was born free, the son of an emancipated slave. He lived, worked, and married in upstate New York, where his family resided. Northrup was a multifaceted laborer and also an accomplished violin player.

Then in 1841, two con men offered Northrup lucrative work playing the fiddle in a circus. So he traveled with them to Washington, D.C., where he was drugged, kidnapped, and sold as a slave into the Red River region of Louisiana. For the next twelve years he survived as the human property of several different slave masters. Most of his years of slavery were under the cruel ownership of a southern planter named Edwin Epps. In 1853, Northup was finally freed by Northern friends who came to his rescue. He returned home to his family in New York and wrote about his experience in *12 Years a Slave*.

Slavery is a horrible evil that was finally abolished in the United States in 1864 under the Emancipation Proclamation. But another form of slavery still haunts millions of people: spiritual slavery. People who never give their lives to Christ can be considered spiritual slaves. You could be one of those people. You could be living in slavery today because you have never committed your heart to Christ. "You shall know the truth, and the truth shall set you free." Some people are still spiritual slaves in spite of the fact that they have given their lives to Christ. Why? Because they see God as a slavemaster, a harsh taskmaster who is eager to hand out punishment. They do not see Him as a loving Father who is eager to demonstrate His love.

This is why making space for grace is crucial to your spiritual life. Grace does more than save you. Grace transforms you. Grace empowers all meaningful change in your life: the power to change your marriage, the power to overcome addictions, the power to deal with tough circumstances. Grace transforms us when we grasp the truth of our true identity.

MORPHING HAPPENS WHEN WE UNDERSTAND OUR IDENTITY

Romans 8:14-17, "For all who are led by the Spirit of God are children of God. So you have not received a spirit that makes you fearful slaves. Instead, you received God's Spirit when he adopted you as his own children. Now we call him, "Abba, Father." For his Spirit joins with our spirit to affirm that we are God's children. And since we are his children, we are his heirs. In fact, together with Christ we are heirs of God's glory. But if we are to share his glory, we must also share his suffering."(NLT)

TWO VIEWS OF GOD

If you're a Christian, you likely see God in one of two ways.

If you see yourself as God's slave, you will be locked in the status quo, unable to morph and change. Slavery leaves people beaten down, discouraged, and demoralized. Slavery treats people as if they are not human and destroys their humanity. If you see yourself as a slave of God, you will struggle to overcome your addictions. You'll find a breakthrough in your relationships an uphill battle. You might be stuck where you are for the rest of your life.

On the other hand, you may see yourself as a child of God. It's impossible to overstate the difference. If you see yourself as a child of God, you have a new heart, a heart in love with God. A heart that's motivated to change. A heart with the power to change. A heart that enables you to beat your addictions. A heart that changes your relationships. A heart that is able to morph.

Which of these two describes you? Paul says that those who are led by the Spirit of God are the children of God. We're not controlled by the sinful nature, we're controlled by the Spirit. We're not obligated to the sinful nature, we're obligated to the Spirit. And when we are led by the Spirit of God, two things happen.

WE MOVE FROM FEAR TO FAITH

With Christ, instead of living with a spirit of fear, we live with the Spirit of God. Instead of living with a spirit of fear, we live with the Spirit of adoption. Now don't misunderstand, there is such a thing as a healthy fear of God. But this is not the same thing as being left with a crippling sense of fear. Let me ask you: How do you view your relationship with God? Do you think of God as your father or as a tyrant? A slavemaster or your friend?

Some people come with shuffling feet into the presence of God. They're afraid He's going to beat them down with accusations and criticism. They see Him as a cruel taskmaster who loves to crack the whip over His servants. But God isn't that way at all. He's a loving, caring Father who embraces us. 1 John 4:18 says, "There is no fear in love, for perfect love casts out fear." (NIV) Being a child of God means we can move from confidence to fear.

The Holy Spirit gives us confidence that God will not disown us when we sin. God doesn't kick us to the curb when we sin. God doesn't love us any less when we sin. We're His son, His daughter, His child. He's wounded by our sin, but He doesn't disown us.

Let's revisit the story of the prodigal son, but instead of examining the heart of the older brother, let's look at the relationship between the younger brother and his father. The younger son comes to his father and demands his inheritance. In so many words, he tells his dad he wishes he was dead. The dad gives him the inheritance his son asks for, and the son goes off and wastes the money on booze and prostitutes. In a short time, he ends up with the pigs in the pigpen. It's there that the younger son has a change of heart. He decides to go home. He's humbled and ready to beg for a chance to be a servant. But when he returns, his dad shocks him and says, No begging, son. We're going to have a party!

Was the dad in Jesus' story heartbroken? Of course. He was devastated. But did he stop loving or disown his son? Of course not. During the heartbreaking days when his son was living in a pigpen, the prodigal's father loved him as much as he ever had!

God loves you just as you are, not as you think you should be! He'd rather die than be without you, and He proved it with His actions. If you don't believe this, you've invented a God who doesn't exist!

We are stalked by insecurity and fear of rejection. Our culture is founded on power, performance, beauty, money, and if we don't fit in, we don't measure up. Husbands reject wives and wives reject husbands. Parents reject their children and children walk away from their parents. The sad fact is that it's getting tougher to find secure and permanent relationships. But grace says God will never reject you because grace means there's nothing you can ever do to make God love you more and nothing you can ever do to make God love you less. You can say with confidence that God will never disown you.

Martin Luther was a German monk who lived a tormented life because he had no assurance of peace about his relationship with God. He lived in constant fear of God. "If I could believe that God was not angry with me, I would stand on my head for joy." Every time Luther thought about Jesus, he envisioned him as a stern judge, condemning him for his sin. Because of this, Luther lived with an unbearable burden of fear and guilt. He couldn't grasp how anyone could be seen as righteous by God. But one day Luther's fear turned to joy.

"I greatly longed to understand Paul's epistle to the Romans, and nothing stood in the way but that one expression, 'the righteousness of God... ' My situation was that, although an impeccable monk, I stood before God as a sinner troubled in conscience ... Therefore I did not love a righteous and angry God but rather hated and murmured against him ... Then I grasped that the righteousness of God is that righteousness by which, through grace and sheer mercy, God justifies us by faith. Thereupon I felt myself to be reborn and to have gone through open doors into paradise ... whereas the righteousness of God had filled me with hate, now it became to me inexpressibly sweet in greater love. This passage of Paul became to me a gateway to heaven."[25]

Knowing that God won't disown us changes everything. It changes us. We gain a totally different outlook on ourselves and our relationship with God. Instead of reporting for duty, we look for ways to serve. Instead of resenting our master, we love our father. Instead of feeling defeated by our failure, we know that we're loved no matter what. So we feel free to start again. Instead of waiting for the gestapo to bark orders, we look to our father for gentle guidance.

But how does this happen? The Holy Spirit gives us confidence that God will not disown us when we sin. And the Spirit gives us confidence to face tough circumstances and live beyond the "what-ifs." What if the economy takes a nosedive? What if they fire me, if I get sick, if an accident happens? What if I don't find a spouse, a house, a job, a friend? What if a certain individual or political party gets elected? What if someone steals my money or breaks into my house?

The voice of fear can easily dominate our lives. We must choose to listen to the voice of the Holy Spirit: "You are a child of God, and God promises to take care of you." Matthew 6:31 tells us, "So do not worry, saying, 'What shall we eat?' or 'What shall we wear?' For the pagans run after all these things, and your heavenly Father knows that you need them." (NIV) Jesus says our Father knows what we need even before we ask Him. He adopted us into His family and will make sure we have everything we need.

Ephesians 1:17-20 says, "I keep asking that the God of our Lord Jesus Christ, the glorious Father, may give you the Spirit of wisdom and revelation, so that you may know him better. I pray that the eyes of your heart may be enlightened in order that you may know the hope to which he has called you, *the riches of his glorious inheritance in his holy people*, and his incomparably great power for us who believe. That power is the same as the mighty strength he exerted when he raised Christ from the dead and seated him at his right hand in the heavenly realms." (NIV)

Tim Keller uses this illustration. Imagine that you're a billionaire, and you have three ten-dollar bills in your wallet. You get out of a cab, and you hand the driver one of the bills for an eight-dollar fare. Later in the day you look in your wallet and find only one ten-dollar bill. You say to yourself, *Either I dropped a ten-dollar bill somewhere, or I gave the taxi driver two bills.*

What are you going to do? Are you going to get upset? Are you going to let the loss ruin the rest of your day? No, you're going to shrug. You're a billionaire. You lost ten dollars. So what? You're too rich to be concerned about an insignificant ten dollar loss.[26]

We must learn to look at life this way. This week, somebody may criticize us. Something we bought or invested in may become less valuable than before. Something we want to happen may not go the way we want it to. Someone we count on may let us down. These are all real, painful losses.

But how do we respond? Do we shake our fist? Toss and turn at night? If we're a Christian, do we let circumstances steal our joy? If we do, it's because we don't understand how amazingly rich we are. We must be still and listen to the voice of the Holy Spirit. We must remember our identity. As Christians, we are spiritual billionaires who wring our hands over ten dollar losses. The Holy Spirit is in our life to remind us of our riches and our inheritance in Christ. Our job is to listen to the Holy Spirit.

How can you and I listen better? Through reading and studying the Word. Through prayer. Through worship. Through being in community with other believers. As we give the Holy Spirit the opportunity to speak to us and remind us of all we have in Christ, we move from fear to faith!

WE MOVE FROM INTIMIDATION TO INTIMACY

Paul says that God has adopted us. Galatians 4:7 (NIV) tells us, "Because you are sons, God has sent the Spirit of His Son into our hearts, crying, 'Abba, Father.'"

The Holy Spirit reminds us of our intimacy with the Father.

In Roman culture, when a baby was born and set at the father's feet, the father either picked up the baby or he turned and walked away, rejecting the baby. Maybe he wanted a boy and had a girl; maybe he wanted a girl and had a boy. Maybe he detected some kind of defect that he didn't like. If a baby was unwanted, the parents would expose the child to the elements for the gods to decide his or her fate. Babies were often taken to the marketplace to be abandoned. Often someone would come along and take the child but raise them as a slave or prostitute to serve their needs.

But in Roman society, adoption was unique. First of all, adoption was irrevocable. Secondly, an adopted child's former life was completely wiped out—including all of his or her debts. Third, an adopted child became, in every sense of the word, the full and complete heir of his or her adoptive father. Whatever the father owned belonged equally to his biological children *and* his adopted children.

Anyone who has adopted children (or knows adoptive families) understands this concept. When you adopt a child, he or she becomes your child, no strings attached. A story is told about a man who adopted a little boy who grew into a young man. One of the father's relatives once made the comment, "You love that boy as if he's your own son."

The father replied, "You don't get it. He IS my son."

When God adopts us into His family, we become one of His children. Paul writes to God's adoptees and says: If you have come to know Jesus, your most defining moment isn't the moment a broken human threw you out but the moment a loving God took you in. He picked you out, He picked you up, and He took you home with you.

Many of us have experienced the pain of being dumped. Dumped by a fiancé. Dumped by friends who suddenly disappear or turn their backs. Dumped by a child who shut us out. Dumped by an employer. Dumped by an employee after investing in them and watching them join a competitor and take your customers with them. Dumped by an unfaithful spouse, only to see them win custody of your children. Has any of this ever happened to you?

Pastor and author Jeff Manion tells about a man whose father left the family when the man was two years old. His dad would visit once a year from another city, check into Motel 6, and have his two sons spend the weekend with him. The man painfully described how at the end of the weekend, his six year-old brother hung onto his dad's ankles and tried to keep him from leaving again. Do you know that feeling of abandonment?

> Make a list with two columns:
> SLAVE   CHILD
> Then, list the characteristics of an individual in each status. Finally, celebrate your status as a child of God!

Your most defining moment is not the moment a flawed human turned their back or threw you out but the moment a perfect, loving

God chose you and took you in. If you've heard the whisper of God and responded to the voice of Christ, you need to know He picked you out, He picked you up, and He brought you home. He adopted you because He desires a relationship with you. You are the precious, prized daughter or son of the Creator. Your most defining moments in life are not what happened to you, but what the Creator did for you. Just whisper these words: "God adopted me."

When God adopted you, you became the brother or sister of Jesus Christ. The Father loves you just as much as He loves His own beloved Son! Your brother Jesus took all of the wrath against your sin that you deserved because He loves you more than you can comprehend. You are an heir along with Jesus Christ of all that God has to offer! Then God gave you His Holy Spirit, His DNA. He implanted His heart and mind and passion inside you!

The Holy Spirit reminds you of your intimacy with God through prayer. Did you notice that in Romans 8:15 (ESV) Paul says, "...by whom [the Spirit] we cry, Abba! Father!" The word abba is an intimate word that describes a child's babbling. The word is similar to our words *daddy*, or *papa*. That's how intimate our relationship with God is. We come to God with spirit of intimacy. "What's next, papa? What are we doing to do next, daddy?" I don't mean any disrespect for God by saying that. We need to hallow and revere the name of God. But our relationship with God is like that of a child talking to their loving Father.

Lee Strobel tells this story. Shortly after the Korean War, a Korean woman had an affair with an American soldier, and she got pregnant. He went back to the United States, and she never saw him again. She gave birth to a little girl, who looked different than other Korean children. Her daughter had light-colored, curly hair. In Korean culture, children of mixed race were ostracized. In fact, many women killed their children rather than have them face such harsh rejection.

But this woman didn't make this choice. She raised her little girl as best she could for seven years until the rejection became too much. Then the mother did something that is difficult for us to imagine ever doing. She abandoned her little girl to the streets.

This child was ruthlessly taunted. People called her the ugliest word in the Korean language: *tooki*, alien devil. Soon the little girl drew conclusions about herself based on the way people treated her. For two years she lived in the streets, until she finally made her way to an orphanage.

One day, word came that a couple from America was coming to adopt a little boy. All the children in the orphanage got excited because at least one little boy would have hope. He would finally have a family. This little girl spent the day cleaning up the boys and combing their hair as she wondered which one would be adopted by the American couple.

The next day when the couple came, this is what the girl recalled: "It was like Goliath had come back to life. I saw the man with his huge hands lift up each and every baby. I knew he loved every one of them as if they were his own. I saw tears running down his face, and I knew if they could, they would have taken the whole lot home with them. He saw me out of the corner of his eye. Now let me tell you. I was nine years old, but I didn't even weigh 30 pounds. I was a scrawny thing. I had worms in my body. I had lice in my hair. I had boils all over me. I was full of scars. I was not a pretty sight. But the man came over to me, and he began rattling away something in English, and I looked up at him. Then he took this huge hand and laid it on my face. What was he saying? He was saying, 'I want this child. This is the child for me.'[27]

Paul Faulkner tells about a man who decided to adopt a teenage girl. The girl was trouble with a capital T. One day she came home from school and ransacked the house looking for money. By the time the man got home, she was gone and the house was in shambles. When the man's friends heard about it, they said, "Don't finalize the adoption. Let her go. After all, she's not really your daughter." The man replied, "Yes, I know. But I told her she was."

His reply meant "I made a commitment to her, and I'm not going back on my commitment."

God made a commitment to adopt you by His grace. God doesn't kick you out of the house when you do wrong. God doesn't look at your life with a frosty stare and say, "Sorry, you've made too many mistakes. You've messed up too often. You've used up all of your chances." Once God adopts us into His family, we're given a fresh start—whenever we need it. He doesn't take us into his family one minute and boot us out the next. All of us have probably wondered at one time or another, *If God had it to do all over again, would He choose me? Would He adopt me?*

You may think you've disappointed God so much that He's written you off and given up on you. But with God, no failure is final. God never stops loving you. You never stop being His! You may have already received that new start and know how great it is to be adopted. If so, celebrate God's unconditional love in your life! But if you have never opened your heart to God's love, invite Him to invade that place which is the deepest part of who you are. God wants to give you a new start by adopting you into His family! You'll never be alone again.

PRACTICAL STEP: Monitor your self-talk. What do you say to yourself about yourself? What do you say to yourself about your relationship with God? What do you say to God about your relationship to Him? Eliminate language that a slave would use in relationship to a harsh master. Instead, use language that a child would use with a loving Father.

When our daughter Haley was a college student, she took a course in developmental psychology. One of the tests was administered using a Scantron machine. When the test was completed, Haley received this email from the professor: "Hi Haley, I have to give you some good (and hilarious) news. Jennifer (the person scoring the test) thought the Scantron was broken because she kept running and running your test and it was not scoring it. She ran it a number of times before she realized it was not broken - you just had not missed any! On the multiple-choice section, you did not miss a single question. Impressive!"

Sadly, this didn't characterize me at any level of my educational career. My tests typically revealed wrong answers instead of right ones. But wouldn't it be great if we got those results on God's test? If all of our answers before God were the right answers? The problem is, my answer sheets are all messed up. Full of errors. Full of failures. I have way more failures than successes. And you do, too.

But the good news is that because of grace, God is able to give me a perfect record. God's grace, made possible by the death and resurrection of Christ, means that my past can be completely rewritten! The same is true for you. No matter how defeated you may feel because of your failures, you don't have to stay that way. Because if you put your trust in Christ, your past is forgiven and forgotten.

You may live with a constant sense of failure. You think of the countless times you've promised to honor Christ but failed. Failed promises. Failed relationships. Failed efforts to do the right thing. There are a lot of Fs on your spiritual report card. Maybe you've given up on God because you figured, He's given up on you. But claim the truth of the gospel. Claim the reality that your past can be forgiven, no matter how sullied. Make space for grace!

ACKNOWLEDGEMENTS

To Landon Saunders, whose preaching had a profound impact on my life. To Tom Olbricht, whose teaching introduced me to grace. To Jimmy and Beth Paul, Reid and Michelle Rector, and Dan and Teresa Killebrew, whose grace has always encouraged me.

END NOTES

1 Lewis Smedes, *Shame and Grace: Healing the Shame We Don't Deserve*, (San Francisco, Harper, 1993)

2 Philip Yancey, *What's So Amazing About Grace?* (Grand Rapids: Zondervan, 1997)

3 Larry Crabb, *Connecting*, (Word, 1997)

4 David Seamands, *Healing Grace: Finding Freedom from the Performance Trap*, (Victor Books, 1988)

5 Elyse Fitzpatrick, *Because He Loves Me*, (Crossway, 2010), pp. 87-91

6 Ray Ortlund, "Who Are You Married To?" The Gospel Coalition blog—Ray Ortlund (2-15-15)

7 Carnegie Simpson, *The Fact of Christ*, (Hodder and Stoughton, 1924)

8 Lewis Smedes, *Shame and Grace: Healing the Shame We Don't Deserve*, (San Francisco, Harper, 1993)

9 Brene Brown, *Daring Greatly*, (Penguin Books, 2012)

10 Khaled Hosseini, *The Kite Runner*, (Bloomsbury Publishing, 2011)

11 SecretRegrets.com

12 David Zahl, *Law and Gospel*, (Mockingbird Ministries, 2015)

13 Timothy Keller, *Generous Justice*, (Dutton, 2010), pp. 104-106

14 Joshua Butler, *The Pursuing God*, (Thomas Nelson, 2016), p.100.

[15] John Stott, *The Cross of Christ*, (Downers Grove: Intervarsity, 1986), p. 175

[16] Benjamin Watson, Facebook Post, November 25, 2014

[17] Patricia Raybon, *My First White Friend*, (Penguin Books, 1996)

[18] NBC News, May 29, 2018

[19] Miroslav Volf in Timothy Keller, *Generous Justice* (Dutton, 2010), pp. 104-106

[20] Fleming Rutledge, *The Crucifixion: Understanding the Death of Jesus Christ*, (Grand Rapids, Eerdmans, 2017)

[21] Matt Woodley, "Jesus, Lord of the Cross," Preaching Today Audio

[22] Lennox, John, *Gunning for God* (Lion, 2011), pp.141-142

[23] Adapted from Christopher J.H. Wright, *Salvation Belongs to Our God*, (IVP Academic, 2008), pp. 48-49

[24] David Anderson: *Gracism*, (Downer's Grove, Intervarsity, 2007)

[25] Roland Bainton, *Here I Stand:A Life of Martin Luther*, (Abingdon, 1978), p.65

[26] Tim Keller, *The Two Advocates*, Penguin Group, 2014 Kindle Locations, 242-244

[27] Lee Strobel, "Meet the Jesus I Know," Preaching Today Audio #211